Growing Up in God's Word

Bible Curriculum

"... from childhood you have known the Holy Scriptures..."
(II Timothy 3:15, NKJV)

Women of the Bible

Table of Contents

Introduction

Why teach children the Bible using only the Bible? Can they understand it? Yes! Is it too boring? No! I have taught a children's Bible class on Sunday mornings for over twenty years and have home-schooled my three children, teaching them the Bible in our home. Guess what? Children are a lot smarter than we give them credit for! There are just a few key things to remember in teaching the Bible to children. First, we need to be enthusiastic about the Bible ourselves. If children see that we think the Bible is boring, they will most likely adopt the same opinion. Be excited about opening the word of God together! Second, don't be afraid to tell them you don't know know an answer to their question. There are many things in the Bible that we have questions about; some things we are able to study and find an answer for, others will have to wait until we get to heaven and can ask God. It's okay to let them know you're stumped too, but encourage them to search for the answer with you. Third, set the bar high for them. Please, please, please don't "dumb" the Bible down to "their level". Children can understand a lot through patient explanation and teaching. For example, if you read a hard word in the Bible that they may not be familiar with, stop and ask them what they think it means, then give them a correct definition. Now they have learned a new word and understand the passage you've just read at the same time. Children like to be challenged and to meet our expectations for them.

The method in this curriculum works because it has been tried among many children of different ages, abilities and levels. Here is the best proof I can offer to you: One of my regular Sunday morning students brought a friend to our class one day. She answered a few questions but mostly sat very quietly, absorbing everything that was going on. Later on, the woman that brought her to church said that the little girl told her on the way home that she wanted to come to our Sunday school class every week because we *"actually teach from the Bible"*. This little girl is not "unchurched" by any means; in fact, she regularly attends a denominational megachurch every Sunday. As the scripture says, "Out of the mouths of babes!"

May your children be like Timothy who, *"from childhood has known the holy Scriptures"* (II Timothy 3:15), and may God bless you as you study His word together.

How to Use this Curriculum

Life began in a garden, so we will be using garden references and symbols throughout this curriculum to designate the different activities. Luke 8:11 says that "*the seed is the word of God*". Our hearts are the soil that the seed needs to be planted in. We should desire to cultivate the soil of our hearts and the hearts of our children to receive the word so that it will grow and produce good fruit for our Lord.

"Growing In The Word": Lesson Text & Discussion

This is the most important part of the curriculum – the teaching of God's Word. The lesson text is broken down into manageable sections to be read aloud and then discussed. If children are old enough to read, let them read out loud. If there are several verses to be read as a section, you could take turns reading a couple of verses per person. If it helps your child, let them jot down notes or write down definitions to new words as you discuss the passage. Encourage them to ask questions and ask them leading questions to get them thinking. The discussion section is basically a paraphrasing of what was just read to make sure there is comprehension of the material. Frequently there are questions to be answered during the discussion phase as well. The section of verses often leave off at a "cliffhanger" moment which helps keep the children engaged. You read and discuss and then you're ready to read on to see what happens next. At the end of this section of the curriculum there are review questions. These can be used in several ways: You may ask them at the end of the lesson, at the end of the week for a review, or if you want to have a graded assignment, you can use them as an oral or written quiz.

*A word about translations. It is important to use a reliable and accurate translation. Some dependable ones are KJV, NKJV, ESV and ASV. Many modern translations have compromised the integrity of the Scriptures in trying to put it in "easier to understand" language. **All references in this curriculum are taken from the New King James Version.**

"Putting Down Roots": Memory Work

Memory work should be practiced every day for the entire week. Use whatever method works the best according to your child's learning style. Here is a link with a list of aids for memorizing scripture: http://pryorconvictions.com/memorizing-scripture/ The Psalmist said in Psalm 119:11, "*Thy word have I hid in my heart that I might not sin against Thee.*" I cannot stress enough how important it is to memorize Scripture. In addition to Scripture, sometimes there are other items included in the Memory Work such as lists of things or categories. A challenge to parents: memorize it with your children!

"Farther Afield": Map Work

There are blank maps provided in Appendix A in the back of the book. These may be photocopied for home use with this curriculum. Most lessons have mapping activities to serve as a visual aid of the places you read about in scripture. To be consistent, you may want to follow a system such as: cities – red, countries – green, bodies of water – blue, wilderness or desert areas – brown, lands or regions – yellow. The map work will indicate different places to be located on the map. Locate and label each item.

"Harvest Fun": Games & Activities

There are games and activities for each lesson to help review and reinforce the material that was covered. It is best to read through these at the beginning of the week to see if any planning ahead needs to be done.

"Digging Deeper": Research

This is primarily for the older students who are able to work independently. If your younger children wish to do these assignments with your help, then by all means, let them! It is a good idea to keep a notebook for these written assignments. These assignments are meant to encourage students of the Bible to learn how to study a topic deeper by using other resources to shed light on the subject. Primarily, books and the Internet will be your sources of information so it's important to do two things: 1) Check the reliability of your source, and 2) Check multiple sources; you might find two or more very different theories or opinions. Some good resources to use are Bible commentaries, concordances (such as Strong's), Bible dictionaries, Bible atlases and Bible software. There are many things we run across in the Bible that we would like to know more about. Have fun exploring!

"Food For Thought": Puzzles

There are at least two puzzles with each lesson to, again, provide review and reinforcement or just to have fun! The puzzles may be worked in the book or photocopied. All puzzle answers are provided in the Answer Key in the back of the book.

"Fruits Of Our Labor": Crafts

There are at least two crafts to do with each lesson. They vary in level of difficulty, but are another means of reinforcement of material covered. Crafts are a good activity for the kinesthetic (hands-on) learner as well as a tangible reminder for the visual learner. Please read ahead early in the week to see what materials you may need to gather in advance.

Suggested Schedule

This curriculum is designed to be used five days a week, 30 minutes to 1 hour per day. It is designed to be used with multiple ages with some activities geared toward older children and others geared toward younger. You may use as many or as few of the activities listed as you choose. Please feel free to alter the suggested schedule to fit the time constraints and needs of your family. However, the lesson and memory work portions should be used for all ages.

Begin or end each day's activities with prayer.

- Day 1 – Read "Growing in the Word": Lesson Text and Discussion. Begin "Putting Down Roots": Memory Work assignments.

- Day 2 – Continue memory work, do "Farther Afield": Map Work activities or "Add a Leaf": Words to Know, and "Harvest Fun": Games and Activities.

- Day 3 – Continue memory work, do "Digging Deeper": Research activities, and/or "Food for Thought": Puzzles.

- Day 4 – Continue memory work, do "Fruits of Our Labor": Crafts, or continue working on previous activities.

- Day 5 – Recite memory work, do lesson Review Questions and finish any assignments or activities from the week that time didn't permit.

A Word About Women

When writing about women of the Bible, how do you even begin to choose which ones to write about? There are, of course, the well-known favorites such as Ruth, Esther, and Mary the mother of Jesus. There are also the not-so-nice but well-known bad girls such as Delilah and Jezebel. This study chooses to focus on seventeen women of the Bible who are a mixed bag. Some are familiar, some are more obscure. Some are great examples for us to imitate, some are great examples of what we should *not* be. Incidentally, this is not just a study for young ladies. Our young men need to be taught at a tender age what qualities to look for in a woman (and what to avoid!), and what better place for all young people to learn about those qualities than by looking to the women in the Bible?

Lesson 1: Eve

The First Woman

Text: Genesis 1:26-27; 2:15-25; 3; 4:1-2, 25

"Growing In The Word": Lesson Text & Discussion

Read Genesis 1:26-27. Genesis is the book of beginnings with a lot of "firsts." God created the world and all that is in it in six days and rested on the seventh day. We can read the creation account in Genesis chapter 1. When we get close to the end of the chapter, we read that God created man and woman on the sixth day of creation. These were the first people to ever live on the earth. In whose image did God create man? (In His own image) Verse 26 mentions "Let Us", "In our", etc. God was not alone in creation. There was God the Father, God the Son (Jesus Christ), and God the Holy Spirit. You might have heard this called the trinity, or the Godhead. Man was made in their image, which was the image of God. We're not told the names of the man and woman, nor how God created them, but that is covered in more detail in the next chapter.

Read Genesis 2:15-17. God gave the man work to do. It was not back-breaking work by any means, but it was a job that gave him responsibility and something productive to do each day. What was his job? (His job was to look after the garden and to keep it.) God told the man that every tree that was created was provided to him for food...except just one. Which tree was forbidden to man and why? (The tree of the knowledge of good and evil was forbidden. If he ate of it, he would die.) God had given man everything he needed and could want. The creation was beautiful and satisfying. This one tree was placed in the garden and forbidden because God has always given man a choice. Man can choose to obey the Lord, or he can choose to disobey Him.

Read Genesis 2:18-20. These events are taking place on the sixth day of creation when the Lord created man, woman, and all of the land animals. They are just being explained in more detail in this chapter. As God was in the process of creating everything, He kept referring to His creation as good. What does He see that is *not* good? (The fact that man is alone.) God knows that Adam needs someone who is suitable for him, but He wants Adam to realize it too. God gives Adam another job to do. What is it? (Naming the animals) Would you have liked this job? Adam must have been pretty creative to think up all of those wonderful names for the animals! As animal after animal walks by him to receive its name, what does Adam realize? (None of these animals would make a proper partner for me!)

Read Genesis 2:21-22. Describe the process of God's creation of woman. (God made Adam fall into a deep sleep, then He opened up Adam's side and removed one of his ribs. God closed up Adam's side, then formed woman from the rib taken from Adam.) God performed the first surgery ever!

Read Genesis 2:23-25. What was Adam's reaction to the woman whom God created for him? (He was excited!) Why did Adam say she would be called a woman? (Because she was taken out of man) God not only performed the first surgery ever, He also performed the first wedding ceremony. He brought the woman to the man so the two of them could be joined together as one. From the beginning of time, God provided marriage to be a beautiful union between one man and one woman for life.

Read Genesis 3:1. The serpent is Satan, and he approaches Eve to deceive her. What does "deceive" mean? (To lie to; to trick.) **John 8:44** tells us that Satan is a liar and the father of lies. He starts off by lying to Eve about what God said. God did *not* say they couldn't eat of any tree of the garden. In fact, in Genesis 2:16 He told them that they were to eat freely of every tree in the garden except just one! What was the name of this tree? (The tree of the knowledge of good and evil)

Read Genesis 3:2-3. Does Eve accurately quote God? **Read Genesis 2:16-17** to find out.

Read Genesis 3:4-5. Satan is calling God a liar! He's telling Eve, 1) You *won't* die, and 2) God's just "afraid" you'll be like Him if you eat this fruit, deciding for yourselves what is good and what is evil. What Eve is hearing and seeing and thinking are strongly tempting her.

Read Genesis 3:6. Eve gives in to the three basic temptations that Satan uses on all mankind as described in **I John 2:16**:

- *Lust of the flesh - "good for food"
- Lust of the eyes - "a delight to the eyes"
- Pride of life - "make one wise"

  *Lust – an unlawful or wrong desire

Eve has committed the first sin. She has chosen to disobey God and destroy the perfection He had created for her and her husband. The perfect relationship she had with God is now over. Sin has entered the world. If that wasn't bad enough, Eve then involves her husband Adam in her sin. Adam submits to his wife and eats the forbidden fruit. Sadly, this is backwards. In **Ephesians 5:25** it says that wives are to submit to their husbands, not the other way around. You might wonder why they didn't immediately die like God said they would. First of all, before they sinned, they were immortal which means they would never have experienced physical death. When they ate of the fruit, their bodies began from that moment to grow older and approach a day of physical death. They lived for hundreds of years after this, but they did eventually die a physical death. Second, they died spiritually. That is, they no longer had a perfect relationship with God but were now separated from Him by their sin. God did not lie – He never does!

Read Genesis 3:7. This is one big OOPS! moment. They didn't get the thrill they were looking for about how lofty and wise they would now be. Instead, their eyes are "opened" to how things *really* are and what a terrible thing they've done, and they are ashamed. We sometimes fall into the same trap. We want to do something so bad that we know we shouldn't, but we give in and do it anyway. It usually doesn't take very long for the good feeling to be gone and the bad feeling of "Oh No!" to set in. Adam and Eve had been naked since their creation, and there was no shame in it. Now that sin has entered the world, they are ashamed of being naked and want to cover themselves. What do they try to use to cover themselves? (Fig leaves)

Read Genesis 3:8-11. Adam and Eve hear God walking in the garden and try to hide in their disgrace. Sin separates us from God. Adam and Eve no longer have the same open and close relationship with God that they had before. Sin has now come between them. What question does God ask Adam and Eve? *("Where are you?")* Does God really not know where they are or what they had done? Of course He did! He asks them this question to get them to realize the seriousness of what they had done and to come forward. Hiding would not do them any good.

Read Genesis 3:12. The blame game is now played for the first time. Who does Adam try to blame? (He tries to blame Eve and also God because He gave the woman to Adam.)

Read Genesis 3:13. Who does Eve try to blame? (She tries to blame the serpent for deceiving her.) Does blaming someone else ever excuse you of the wrong you've done? (No) When we have done something wrong, God wants us to confess or admit the sin and take responsibility for it, not blame someone else.

Read Genesis 3:14. How does God curse the serpent? (It is cursed above all animals and will have to crawl on its belly and eat dust.)

Read Genesis 3:15. This is the "mother promise" of the entire Bible. It is the first prophecy of the coming Savior, Jesus Christ. Satan would deal a temporary, but not deadly blow to Jesus by the crucifixion (bruise his heel), but Christ's power over death and the grave through His resurrection would be fatal to Satan (bruise his head). After this first devastating sin, God gives man hope and a promise of salvation for the first time.

Read Genesis 3:16. How was woman cursed? (She will have pain in childbirth, and her husband will rule over her.)

Read Genesis 3:17-19. How was man cursed? (He will have to use hard labor and sweat to bring forth food from the ground, and he will die a physical death [dust to dust].) Adam had to work before sin entered the world, (Remember, he was to "tend the garden"?) but that work didn't require sweating and pain and difficulty. Now, it will. What will grow along with the food that Adam will have to deal with? (Thorns and thistles – ouch!) When God had created Adam, he formed him from the dust of the ground (Genesis 2:7), so that is where he will return when he eventually dies.

Read Genesis 3:20. Adam officially gives his wife a name. What does "Eve" mean? (Mother of all living)

Read Genesis 3:21. Who made Adam and Eve's clothes? (God) What were the clothes made from? (Animal skins) This required the first sacrifice (death).

Read Genesis 3:22. Who is the "Us"? (Father, Son, and Holy Spirit) What would happen if Adam and Eve ate of the tree of life? They would be immortal (again!). The Lord does not want this and will not allow it to happen.

Read Genesis 3:23-24. What was Adam to do now after being sent out of the garden? (Work the ground.) What did God do to make sure they didn't return to the garden to try to eat of the tree of life? (He placed a cherubim and flaming sword as a guard.) What a sad ending to such a happy beginning! However, remember that God doesn't leave them hopeless. They have the promise of a coming Savior - Jesus Christ the Lord!

Read Genesis 4:1-2. Another first for Eve – she gives birth to the first baby ever born and becomes a mother. What was the name of her firstborn son? (Cain) She must have been so excited as she looked at the tiny little figure in her arms. She might have even been excited, wondering if this child was the promised Savior. Why does she say she named him Cain? (She says she had gotten him from the Lord.) What is the name of Eve's second son? (Abel) As these two sons grew, they had different occupations or jobs which they did. What did Cain do? (He was a farmer.) What did Abel do? (He was a shepherd.)

Read Genesis 4:25. By the end of chapter four, Eve has experienced another first – a death of someone she loves. Her firstborn son Cain had killed his brother Abel. What sadness and heartache this first mother must have felt! Not only did she lose her second son, but her firstborn committed the murder. But God continued to bless Eve by giving her another son. What was his name? (Seth) His name means "appointed." Why did Eve give him this name? (She said that God had appointed another seed for her in place of Abel.)

Eve was the first woman who experienced many "firsts" – she became the first wife in the first wedding, the first mother, and the first sinner. She witnessed the first sacrifice and felt the first hope when she heard God give the first promise of salvation.

Review Questions: (Answers are provided in the Answer Key.)

1. On what day was Eve created?

2. Describe how God created Eve.

3. What did Adam say when God brought Eve to him?

4. What two "firsts" did God perform in Genesis 2:21-22?

5. According to John 8:44, who is the father of lies?

6. Of which tree in the garden of Eden were Adam and Eve not to eat?

7. What are the three basic temptations Satan uses on all mankind?

8. What does Ephesians 5:25 tell us that wives are to do?

9. How does sin affect our relationship with God?

10. Who does Adam try to blame for his sin?

11. Who does Eve try to blame for her sin?

12. Why is Genesis 3:15 a very important verse in the Bible?

13. What was Eve's punishment (or curse)?

14. What does Eve's name mean?

15. What was the name of Eve's first son?

16. What was the name of Eve's second son?

17. What happened to her second son?

18. What was the name of Eve's third son?

19. What does his name mean?

20. Name some "firsts" that Eve experienced.

"Putting Down Roots": Memory Work

- Memorize Genesis 2:24

- Memorize Genesis 3:20

- Memorize the 7 days of creation: Day 1-light, Day 2-firmament or air we breathe, Day 3-dry land and green things, Day 4-sun, moon and stars, Day 5-fish and fowl, Day 6-man, woman, and land animals, Day 7-God rested

 ## "Farther Afield": Map Work

Map 1

- Locate Mesopotamia

- Locate the Garden of Eden. Hmmm...We don't know its exact location, but the Bible gives us a few clues. Genesis 2:8 - it was in the east. Genesis 2:11 - a river and land we don't know. Genesis 2:13 - a river and land we don't know. Genesis 2:14 - two rivers, one we know and a country we know. Our best guess would be somewhere in modern day Iraq.

- Locate the Euphrates River

- Locate the country of Assyria

 ## "Harvest Fun": Games & Activities

- Don't Touch that Fruit! - This game can be played like Hot Potato. Use a piece of plastic fruit, or even an actual piece of fruit such as an apple or orange. Stand in a circle and pass the piece of fruit as fast as you can while someone plays music in the background. (This can be some acappella hymns or maybe someone can sing a song about the days of creation!) When the music stops suddenly, whoever is holding the fruit is out. Continue play until one person is left. After playing, discuss the temptation of Eve. The longer she looked at the fruit, the more she was tempted to touch it. Once she touched it, she was tempted to taste it. To successfully fight temptation, it is best to not taste, not touch, and not even look!

- Family Activity Jar – Doing things together as a family creates long-lasting memories and builds stronger relationships. Make a list of different activities that you can do together as a family, cut apart each idea on its own slip of paper, then fold up the slips and place them in a jar labeled "Family Activity Jar". Set aside time one evening a week to pick a slip of paper out of the jar and do the activity. Here are some ideas to get you started: Make s'mores in the back yard; have a picnic in the park; do sword drills to practice using your Bibles; camp out in the back yard; play a favorite board game; make up a song to learn a memory verse together; have a water gun fight; bake cookies together; play a Bible game such as "I'm thinking of a Bible character" or Bible charades; visit the zoo; go on a nature scavenger hunt; have a pillow fight; go geo-caching; put on a play (with costumes and props) of a Bible story; make a family photo tree (see craft section).

- Operation – God performed the first operation when in Genesis 2:21-22 He put Adam into a deep sleep, opened up his side, took out a rib and then closed up his flesh. With that one rib from Adam, God formed a woman. If you have the game "Operation", play a round for fun. Bonus points for the one who successfully removes the ribs! After playing, think about how God made all the beasts of the earth and even Adam from the dust of the ground. Discuss why you think God took a part of Adam to make Eve.

"Digging Deeper": Research

- Satan – Research his origins: Was he a created being? What kind of being was he? Where did he originally dwell? What happened to him? What does the word "Satan" mean? How does John 8:44 describe him?

- Seed of Woman – In Genesis 3:15, God promised Satan that the Seed of woman would crush his head. Jesus was the promised seed who would be victorious over Satan, so Satan tried many times and many ways to destroy the line that Jesus would come through. Read the following scriptures then write a short summary about who tried to kill whom and what the outcome was, including survivors (if known). Exodus 2:15-22, 3:1-10; I Chronicles 21:1-7; II Chronicles 22:10-12; Esther 3:8-9, 4:1-3, 15-17, 7:5-6, 10, 9:1-16; Matthew 2:1-16.

"Food For Thought": Puzzles

- Finish the Family – Eve was the "mother of all living." All of the people and families in the world came from the first family, Adam and Eve. For this puzzle, you will need the "Finish the Family" template in Appendix B. These family units are all in the Bible. Some of them are parents and children, some are brothers or brothers and sisters, and others include grandparents. See if you can correctly finish each family! Print out a copy of the families page, then print out a copy of the fill-in-the-blank names and cut them apart. Place the correct names in the blanks then check your answers to see how you did. The correct answers are located in the Answer Key along with explanations as to how each set of names are related.

- Mystery Math – Use your math skills to answer the following questions. Answers are provided in the Answer Key.

1. On which day of creation was Eve created by God? _____

2. How many children of Eve are named in Genesis 4? _____

   Divide the answer to #1 by the answer to #2. _____

3. How many are included in the Godhead referred to in Genesis 1? _____

   Add the answer to #3 to the last answer to #2. _____

4. How many people ate of the forbidden fruit? _____

   Add the answer to #4 to the last answer to #3. _____

5. On which day of creation would dinosaurs have been created? _____

   Subtract the answer to #5 from the last answer to #4. _____

   What is the final number? _____ God said that when a man and a woman were joined together in marriage, they would be _____. (Genesis 2:24)

"Fruits Of Our Labor": Crafts

- Creation Mural - To make a mural, take a large piece of poster board or butcher paper and draw or paint a creation scene that includes something from each day of creation. (Don't forget Adam and Eve!)

- Tree of Knowledge of Good and Evil – Use modeling clay (such as Sculpey) to form a tree of the knowledge of good and evil. Make the fruit very colorful and appealing. Remember, Eve thought it looked good enough to eat, and sadly, she did.

- Family Photo Tree – A family is a special blessing from God. Spend some quality family time by working on this fun craft project together. You will be making a family photo tree that will display some of your favorite photos in a fun and decorative way. For this craft you will need: A plain flowerpot, colored rocks, a fake white tree branch (or small real branches), and pictures. To make this family photo tree, the first thing you will need is photos! Pick several photos that you may want to use and then let each person pick a couple of their favorites. The

© 2018, Pryor Convictions Media, Paul & Heather Pryor, St. Petersburg, FL

number of photos you use will depend on how much branch space you have available. Find pictures that remind you of good times together with people in your family – holidays, silly pictures, etc. Cut the photos out in leaf shapes. (There is a leaf template page available in Appendix B if you would like to use it.) Next, use paint, sharpie markers, stickers, or another art medium of your choice to write your family name on the flowerpot. Then decorate the rest of the flowerpot if you would like. Now, prepare your tree! Place your colored rocks in the flowerpot and anchor your branch(es). If it is not secure enough, hot glue can be placed in the bottom of the pot to secure the branches, then fill with rocks after the glue has dried. Next, start placing your photos all over the tree. There are a few ways you can do this: glue dots, double stick tape, or hole punch one end of each picture and run string or twistie ties through the hole then tie it or wrap it around a branch. After all of the pictures are "branched", find a place to place your family photo tree where it can be viewed and enjoyed each day. This would also make a nice gift for family members who may live far away such as grandparents.

Lesson 2: Jochebed

A Woman Who was a Brave Mother

Text: Exodus 2:1-10; Acts 7:20-23

"Growing In The Word": Lesson Text & Discussion

Read Exodus 2:1. In this verse, we learn that a man and woman get married, but we are not told their names. We are also told which tribe of Israel they were both from. The nation of Israel was divided into 12 tribes which represented the 12 sons of Jacob. Which tribe were these two people from? (The tribe of Levi) We can find out their names by reading **Exodus 6:20.**

Read Exodus 2:2. This man and woman, Amram and Jochebed, had a baby boy. How is he described? (A beautiful child) This was not, however, their first child. Amram and Jochebed had two other children, a daughter named Miriam (whose name is first mentioned in Exodus 15:20) and another son named Aaron. The baby's name is not given in this verse, but we will see later that it is Moses. **Read Exodus 7:7.** How much older than Moses was Aaron? (Aaron was three years older.) When this baby was born, his mother did something unusual with him until he was three months old. What did Jochebed do? (She hid the baby.) This may seem like a very strange thing to do, but Jochebed had a very good reason for doing this. She was trying to protect her little son from the cruel ruler of Egypt. When the book of Exodus opens, we read in chapter 1 how the ruler of Egypt, called Pharaoh, made all of the Israelite people slaves. He made them work very hard doing all kinds of labor. They had to make bricks for building, serve in the fields, and do anything else they were commanded to do. The Pharaoh was afraid of the Israelites because there were so many of them. He thought that by making them his slaves, he could keep them under his control. One of the terrible things he did to keep them from growing in number was to issue a command concerning all the baby boys born to the Israelite (or Hebrew) women. **Read Exodus 1:22** to find out what this command was. Can you imagine how terrible and heartbreaking this must have been to the Israelite families? If you had been an Israelite mother or father living in Egypt at this time, and you were expecting a new baby to be born soon, how would you feel? When Jochebed gave birth to her beautiful little boy, she could not and would not obey the wicked command of the Pharaoh. **Read Hebrews 11:23.** Jochebed and her husband were not afraid of the king's command because they had faith in someone who was mightier. They believed and trusted in God.

Read Exodus 2:3-4. After three months, Jochebed was in a difficult position. She was finding it impossible to hide her baby successfully. Babies sleep a lot when they are first born, but as they grow, they start to make lots of noises - squealing, babbling, and of course, crying. Jochebed continues to show how strong and brave she is and how much she trusts in God. What does she make for the baby? (She makes a little ark of bulrushes.) Do you remember the Bible story of Noah and the ark? Noah used wood for the enormous ark that would house numerous animals, provisions, and his own family, but Jochebed simply weaves together some bulrushes which was a reedy plant that grew by the river. She and Noah both made their arks waterproof by applying a thick tar-like substance called pitch or bitumen. When the little ark was all finished and waterproofed, Jochebed carefully laid her little son in it. Where did she place the little ark? (She put in the river near the water's edge in the reeds.) She didn't simply blow him a kiss, say goodbye, and leave him. She left someone there to keep watch over him and to see what would happen. Who was it? (The baby's sister) This would be Miriam, and while she was still young at this time, she was someone who was responsible and trustworthy enough for her mother to give her such an important task.

Read Exodus 2:5. Who came down to the river to bathe? (The daughter of Pharaoh) While she was in the water, she had some of her maids or attendants nearby walking along the riverbank. The princess spotted the little ark floating in the water among the reeds and was curious. What did she command one of her maids to do? (She sent her to get the ark out of the water.) Remember that the baby's sister was hiding close by and watching all of this. Do you think she was glad her baby brother had been found or fearful? (Discuss.)

Read Exodus 2:6-8. What did the baby do when the ark was opened up? (He cried.) As the daughter of Pharaoh, do you think it was likely that she knew the command of her father to throw the Hebrew baby boys into the river? But when she saw this little baby, she had compassion on him, even though she knew he was a Hebrew and not an Egyptian. Compassion is strong feelings of pity and sympathy with a desire to do something to help. This princess wasn't cruel like her father. She saw a sweet, helpless little baby crying, and her heart reached out to him. Miriam saw her chance and boldly came forward with an offer. What did she ask Pharaoh's daughter? (She asked her if she would like her to go and find a Hebrew nurse for the child.) Miriam knew that the princess would not be taking care of feeding the child herself but would require a woman to nurse him and take care of him while he was still very little. Did the princess take her up on her offer? (Yes) Of course, Miriam went straight back to her mother and brought her back to Pharaoh's daughter to accept the position. Can you imagine what Jochebed must have felt like when her daughter came and reported everything that had happened? Not only was her precious baby safe, but he would continue to be protected, and she would get to take care of him!

Read Exodus 2:9-10. When Jochebed was brought before Pharaoh's daughter, she was given her instructions. What was she to do, and what would the princess do? (Jochebed was to take the child home with her and nurse him and care for him, and the princess would pay her for being the baby's nurse.) Not only would Jochebed be allowed to take of her son without fearing for his life, she was actually going to be paid for doing it. Jochebed was going to be allowed to raise her son for a few years until he is old enough to be presented to the Pharaoh's daughter and become her adopted son. She will use these years wisely by teaching her child exactly who he is and who God is. When the child was old enough, Jochebed brought him to Pharaoh's daughter. She took him to be her own son, raising him as an Egyptian and giving him all the privileges of being a prince of Egypt. Why did she give him the name Moses? (She named him Moses because the name means "drawn out." She drew him out of the water at three months old.)

Read Acts 7:20-23. This passage of scripture comes from part of a sermon that a man named Stephen was preaching to the Jewish leaders in the Sanhedrin. He was giving them a history lesson about their ancestors and part of it contained these verses about the life of Moses. They describe most of what we have just read and studied, but they also add a little more information. First, how does verse 22 describe Moses? (He was taught the wisdom of the Egyptians and was a man mighty in words and deeds.) This shows us that Moses was given an education and trained up as an Egyptian. He lived as the son of Pharaoh's daughter meaning he lived in the royal palace, not in the Hebrew slave quarters. He would have been surrounded by wealth, not poverty, and he would have been trained and taught the kinds of things Egyptian princes were supposed to know, not working out under the hot sun in the fields all day. As a prince of Egypt, do you think he would have been taught about the one true God or would he be taught about the many gods and goddesses of Egypt? (Discuss) Yet, we see in verse 23 that he knew all along that he was a Hebrew. When he was a grown man, he wanted to go visit *"his brethren"*, the Israelites. How would he know this? His mother (and father) had taught him. Remember how faithful his parents were, not fearing the king's command? These same faithful parents taught their little boy all about God. Thanks to the teaching and care of his mother, Moses knew exactly where he came from and how God had preserved his life. She must have told him that he was special and that God had a wonderful purpose for him. The Israelites had been praying to God for years, pleading to be set free from their terrible bondage of slavery. Moses was to be the answer to that prayer as God used him many years later to lead his people out of Egypt.

Jochebed is a wonderful example of a brave and godly mother. She trusted in God and did not fear Pharaoh. As a result, she was the mother of one of the greatest leaders of God's people - the one who led God's people out of Egyptian slavery, the one who gave God's law to the people, and the one who led the nation of Israel to the promised land of Canaan.

<u>Review Questions</u>: (Answers are provided in the Answer Key.)

1. What tribe of Israel were Amram and Jochebed from?

2. How many children did they have, and what were their names?

3. Why did the Pharaoh of Egypt make the Israelites slaves?

4. What terrible command did the Pharaoh issue in Exodus 1:22?

5. What unusual thing did Jochebed do with her baby boy for the first three months after he was born?

6. What materials did Jochebed use to fashion a little waterproof ark for her baby?

7. After the baby was placed inside, where was the ark placed?

8. Who remained close by to watch over the baby and to see what would happen?

9. Why did the daughter of Pharaoh come down to the river?

10. When her maid brought her the ark and opened it, what did the baby do?

11. What was the reaction of the princess to this?

12. What did Miriam boldly offer the princess?

13. Who was selected for this position?

14. What does the name Moses mean?

15. Did Moses realize he was a Hebrew?

 "Putting Down Roots": Memory Work

- Memorize the 12 tribes of Israel: Reuben, Simeon, Levi, Judah, Gad, Asher, Naphtali, Dan, Issachar, Zebulun, ½ tribe of Manasseh (son of Joseph), ½ tribe of Ephraim (son of Joseph), Benjamin

- Memorize Hebrews 11:23

"Farther Afield": Map Work

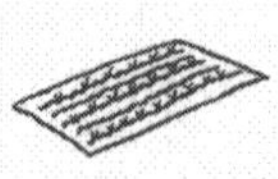

Map 2

- Locate the country of Egypt

- Locate the Nile River

- Locate the land of Goshen

 "Harvest Fun": Games & Activities

- Find Baby Moses – Take a small basket or container and place a tiny baby doll inside. (You can find tiny ones in cake decorating sections of craft stores.) Take turns hiding baby Moses somewhere in the house or even outside. Let other players try to find baby Moses. You can help them with "hot" or "cold" clues.

- Scripture Scramble - This game is for two players or two teams. Before play begins, you will need index cards in two different colors. Write out Hebrews 11:23, one word per card, in each color. Let one person who is not playing the game hide all of the cards around a large room or throughout a house. When "Go" is called, the two players or two teams will race to find all of the index cards in their assigned color, then see how quickly the verse can be correctly assembled. The player or team who correctly assembles the verse first is the winner. This is an "open book" game so feel free to use your Bibles, but if you want to make it more challenging, do this from memory (after all, this is one of your memory verses for this lesson!).

"Digging Deeper": Research

- The Nile River – The ark containing baby Moses was placed in the Nile River. Research some facts about this famous Egyptian river. Specifically, what importance did this river have in ancient Egypt, and what kind of animals lived in it? How would this make it even more dangerous for the baby Moses to be left floating in this river?

- Moses' Family Tree – Jochebed was from the tribe of Levi as well as her husband Amram. Trace their family tree back to Levi who was one of the twelve sons of Jacob. (Read Exodus 6:16-20) How were Jochebed and Amram related? Besides Moses, what were the names of their other children? (Read Exodus 7:1, 15:20) How much older than Moses was his brother? (Read Exodus 7:7)

"Food For Thought": Puzzles

- Word Scramble with Clues – Read the following clues to help you unscramble the letters to form the correct answer, then write it on the line. Answers are provided in the Answer Key.

1. v e i l – Tribe of Israel that Moses was from _____
2. s h r e w b e – The name of God's people _____
3. d e b c h o j e – The name of Moses' mother _____
4. m a r m a – The name of Moses' father _____
5. t h e r a u g d – This relative of Pharaoh found Moses _____
6. r a m i m i – She watched over her baby brother _____
7. b l u e s r u h s – What Moses' mother used to weave a basket _____
8. i f l u b e a t u – How Moses was described as a baby _____

9. e r h e t – How many months old Moses was when placed in the river _____

10. i t f a h – Moses' parents had this when they hid him from Pharaoh _____

- What's Wrong with this Picture? - Read the following account from this lesson. Some of the statements are incorrect! Cross out any words or phrases that are incorrect and write the correct information above it. Answers are provided in the Answer Key.

A man from the tribe of Levi took as a wife a daughter of Judah. They had a beautiful little boy whom they hid from Pharaoh for four months. When his mother could no longer hide him, she made a small ark of pine needles and daubed it with pitch. She placed the baby in the basket and placed him in the Red Sea. His brother stood nearby to see what would happen. The daughter of Pharaoh came down to the water to wash her clothes, and she saw the basket. One of her maids brought it to her, and when she opened it, the baby laughed. The baby's brother asked her if she would like a doctor for the child, and she said, "Yes." The baby's real mother was chosen to nurse him, then he was brought to Pharaoh's daughter to become her son. She named him Moses which means he was taken out of a basket.

"Fruits Of Our Labor": Crafts

- Basket Weaving – Moses' mother, Jochebed, wove a basket out of bulrushes to lay her baby in. Try your hand at a basket weaving technique by making a mini colored-paper basket. You will need colored construction paper (you may want to use more than one color), clear tape, scissors, rubber band, and an empty paper towel roll. Cut the construction paper into 5 ¼" by 2 ½" strips. Fold each strip lengthwise to about an inch wide. Start by making the basket's base: lay two strips in the shape of a plus sign and tape them together. Add four crosspieces to form an asterisk, securing with tape. *If you'd like a taller basket, tape extra strips to the ends of each of these in the base. Center the paper towel roll in the middle of the strips. Turn upside down and fold all of the strips down over the roll and secure with a rubber band toward the top edge of the strips to hold them in place. Then starting at the base of the basket, tuck one folded paper strip under one paper rib and secure with tape. Begin weaving around the form, pulling tightly as you go. Tape the end in place. Continue adding strips and weaving until you reach the height of basket you want. Leave about 1 - 1 ½ inches unwoven at the top. Remove the rubber band and take the basket off of the paper towel roll. Fold the top edges down inside the basket and tape.

- Salt dough map - Make the following salt dough recipe and use it to make a map of the land of Egypt. You may want to make and enlarge a copy of Map 2 from Appendix A to lay your salt dough on. To make the salt dough, blend 1 cup salt with 2 cups of flour. Gradually add in enough water to make a slightly sticky dough. If you want to color your dough, divide it up and work in a few drops of food coloring or tempera paint, or you can use plain dough and paint it with tempera paints after it has dried. Tape or glue your map on a sturdy base then place your salt dough on the map. You may want to build up portions where there are higher elevations, then place rivers and seas in their correct locations. When you are finished, let your map dry overnight. The following day, paint your map if needed, then label the Nile River, the land of Goshen, and the cities of Pithom and Raamses, which were the two supply cities that Pharaoh ordered the Hebrew slaves to build.

Lesson 3: Rahab
A Woman of Faith

Text: Joshua 2

"Growing In The Word": Lesson Text & Discussion

You may remember the famous Bible event of the Israelites marching around the city of Jericho for seven days, with its mighty wall finally crashing and crumbling to the ground. Well, before any marching began, a few other interesting and important events took place first, some of which involved a woman named Rahab.

Read Joshua 2:1. At this point in Israel's history, Moses has recently died, and Joshua is now the leader of the people. They have arrived at the promised land of Canaan and are preparing to enter the land and conquer it as God had told them to do. If you look at a map of the land (see Appendix A, Map 4), you will see a line going up the middle which is the Jordan River. The land of Canaan that God had promised to Israel was located on the west side (left) of the river. In this verse, the Israelites are encamped on the east side (right) of the Jordan River in Acacia Grove across from the city of Jericho which is going to be the first city they attempt to conquer. Before any soldiers start gearing up, Joshua is going to send out some spies to view the land and the city of Jericho itself. How many spies does he send out? (Two) Once the spies enter the city, they don't want to attract any attention to themselves but rather would like to appear as a couple of regular travelers. Whose house do they go to for lodging? (Rahab) This woman is referred to as a harlot. Harlots were considered sinful women because they did things with their bodies that God only allows in the state of marriage. We will see in this lesson how God can have a powerful effect on the heart of any sinner and use them for His purposes and glory.

Read Joshua 2:2-3. Someone in the city saw these two men and were very suspicious. This person went to the king to inform him that spies from Israel were inside their city. What does the king of Jericho do with this information? (He sends a message to Rahab to produce these men.) What do you think the king was planning to do to these two spies? (Answers will vary.) Whatever it was, it would not have been good! Rahab is faced with a tough choice: will she obey her king and turn over the spies to him, or will she protect these two men who are spying out her hometown in order to destroy it?

Read Joshua 2:4-7. What was Rahab's choice? (She hid the spies and protected them from the king.) Where did she say the men were? (She said they had left the city at night and might be overtaken if pursued quickly.) Rahab had, in fact, hidden the spies in a very ingenious place – she hid them on her roof underneath some stalks of drying flax. Stalks of flax were cut and bundled together, looking a little like shocks of wheat. Rahab must have had several of these on her roof in order to conceal two men under them. Meanwhile, the men of Jericho were (so they thought) hot on the trail of the Israelite spies. They went all the way to the fords of the Jordan but had no luck. The fords were shallow crossing places in the river.

(*Note to parents/teachers: It may come up that Rahab told a lie in order to protect the spies and lying is supposed to be wrong. Right? I love when kids put their thinking caps on! This is a tough one to answer, even for adults, but here are some things to consider: 1) Lying is a sin. Period. However, the Bible shows us that no one is perfect, and there were those who sometimes made a bad or wrong decision even when it was supposed to be for a "greater good." The Bible gives us several examples of this happening, but it never condones the sin itself. 2) There were occasions when a person or persons would seem to be justified in telling a lie to save their own life or someone else's, yet they did not, and God provided a way of escape for them. (For example, Daniel, Shadrach, Meshach & Abednego) 3) Rahab was not an Israelite who had studied the law of Moses, but was a heathen living in a pagan nation. In the Old Testament, there were "times of ignorance" which "God winked at." The bottom line is that lying is always a sin. "A lying tongue" is one of the six things that God hates. Proverbs 6:17)

Read Joshua 2:8-11. After the men of Jericho had left, Rahab went up on the roof and had an interesting conversation with the two spies. What did she say she knew the Lord had given them? (The land) This is an amazing thing to say! Rahab lives in a place that worships idols, not the one true and living God. Yet, she knows who the Israelites are, who their God is, and that the land of Canaan will be theirs. According to her, how do the people of Jericho and the entire land of Canaan feel about the Israelites? (They are terrified of them.) This is amazing as well. When you read about the city of Jericho, you learn that not only was the city huge, it was surrounded by a wall that was so thick, at least one chariot could have driven around the top of it. The Israelites were a nation of people who had been slaves in Egypt, then wandered in the wilderness for 40 years. They had no permanent home. They had no fancy, advanced military equipment, no chariots or battering rams. They were just a bunch of foot soldiers with hand-held weapons. Yet, everyone in the land of Canaan was quaking in their boots because of them! Why was this? Rahab explained why by listing all of the things God had done for His people that everyone far and wide had heard about. What were the things she mentioned? (The parting of the Red Sea and the destruction of the two kings of the Amorites – Sihon and Og) She continued by saying no one among them had any courage to stand against Israel. Then Rahab said another amazing thing – she acknowledged that the Lord is God, of heaven above and earth beneath. Rahab's statement shows that she had faith. She had heard about the God of Israel, she believed in His power and might, and she proclaimed Him to be Lord of all. This amazing faith is what motivated her to protect the Israelite spies and what motivates her to ask them for a very big favor.

Read Joshua 2:12-14. What does Rahab ask the spies to do for her? (She wants them to spare her life and the lives of her family when the Israelites conquer the city. Do the spies agree to this? (Yes) But there is a condition – they tell her that she and her family must keep quiet about them and their mission. If they do, then they promise her that she and her family will be treated kindly when the Israelites take the land.

Read Joshua 2:15-21. Now the spies have to get out of Jericho without being detected. They can't just walk out of Rahab's front door because everyone in the city is on the lookout for them. Rahab has the solution to that problem. What does she do? (She lets them down by a rope hanging out of her window.) Rahab's house is located on the city wall so the spies are in a good position to make their escape. Before they go, Rahab warns them to go hide in the mountains while the men of Jericho are still trying to track them down. How long does she say they should hide themselves? (Three days) After this, it should be safe for them to come out of hiding and return to their camp. The spies have a final message for her as well. They remind her of their promise to her and that they will keep it, but they want her to do two things. What are they? (1-She needs to tie a scarlet cord in the window of her house, identifying it as hers, and 2-She needs to bring all of her family that she wants to be saved from destruction into her house.) What will happen if any of these instructions are not followed? (The spies won't be bound to their promise to her, and anyone who goes outside of her house will not be protected from harm or death.) The spies also tell her that if she *does* follow all of their instructions, yet harm comes to anyone in her family, then they will personally be responsible for it and will pay for it. Did Rahab agree to everything that the spies said? (Yes) As soon as she let them down the rope, and they disappeared into the night, what did Rahab do? (She tied the scarlet cord in her window, just as they had told her to do.)

Read Joshua 2:22-24. Where did the spies go after leaving the house of Rahab? (They went and hid in the mountains.) They followed her advice exactly and hid for three days. It was a good thing they did, because the men of Jericho were still searching for the spies everywhere. When the coast was clear, the spies came down out of the mountains and "crossed over." This means they crossed the Jordan River to go back to the Israelite camp. When they arrived in the camp, who did they go and report to? (Joshua) Give a brief summary of their report. (They told Joshua that everyone in the country was terrified of them, and that the Lord was going to give them success in taking the land.)

Read Joshua 6:25. The rest of the story...When Israel, under the leadership of Joshua, went into the land of Canaan and conquered the city of Jericho, we see that the promises of the spies and of Rahab were kept. She and her family were spared because she showed kindness to the spies and protected them. This is a happy ending, but the story actually doesn't end here. Make sure you do the research project about Rahab to see what else happened to her and how important she was in the history of the Israelites and what connection she had to Jesus.

Rahab gives us a great example of faith. She was a woman with a bad reputation, a sinner living in a city of idolatrous people who did not follow the Lord. Yet, when she heard of the mighty works of God, she believed in Him as the one true God and wanted to help His people. As a result of her faith, her life and the lives of her family were spared from destruction. **Hebrews 11:31** tells us, *"By faith the harlot Rahab did not perish with those who did not believe, when she had received the spies with peace."*

Review Questions: (Answers are provided in the Answer Key.)

1. How many spies did Joshua send out to view the land?

2. On which side of the Jordan River were the Israelites encamped at this time?

3. Who was informed that there were spies in the city staying at the house of Rahab?

4. What did he do with this information?

5. Where did Rahab say the spies were?

6. Where did Rahab hide the spies?

7. How far did the men of Jericho go in trying to track down the spies?

8. How did Rahab describe the feelings of the people of Jericho and all of Canaan concerning the Israelites?

9. Rahab told the spies that she had heard what the God of Israel had done for His people. What three events did she mention?

10. What request did Rahab make of the spies?

11. Did the spies agree to her request?

12. How did the spies leave Jericho without detection?

13. How long did Rahab tell the spies to hide in the mountains?

14. What two conditions did the spies give Rahab in order for them to keep their promise to her?

15. What condition would allow the spies to break this promise?

16. Did Rahab agree to everything the spies told her to do?

17. What did Rahab do as soon as the spies left her home?

18. Where did the spies go after leaving Rahab's house?

19. When they returned to the Israelite camp, whom did they report to?

20. Give a brief summary of their report.

21. When Joshua and the Israelites conquered the city of Jericho, were the promises by Rahab and the spies kept?

22. What New Testament verse tells us that Rahab acted in faith?

 "Putting Down Roots": Memory Work

- Memorize Joshua 6:25

- Memorize Hebrews 11:31

- Memorize James 2:25

 "Farther Afield": Map Work

Map 3

- Locate the Red Sea

- Locate Acacia Grove (also known as Abel Shittim)

- Locate the Jordan River

- Locate the city of Jericho

 "Harvest Fun": Games & Activities

- Hide the Spies! - Rahab hid the Israelite spies in a rather unique spot – on her roof under stalks of flax. Take turns being a spy or two spies (if there are enough players) and hide. When "Go" is called, let the other players try to discover the spies' hiding place. Another way this could be played is to use two small action figures to represent the two spies. Let one person hide them, then let the other players try to find them in a two minute time frame. Hot and cold clues may be given to assist the seekers.

- "I Spy" - In this lesson, we read about two spies who were sent on a mission. While we're not going to spy out any enemy territory, it still might be fun to play a game of "I Spy." There are two versions from which to choose: 1) Things in nature – Go outside or to a park or zoo, etc. and take turns "spying" something outdoors. Let other players try to guess what it is you're spying by asking you yes or no questions. The Israelite spies were not just spying on the city of Jericho but on the surrounding land as well. 2) People/Things in the Bible – Play the same way, only "spy" on a Bible character or Bible thing (such as an altar, the ark, Mt. Sinai, etc.).

After playing one or both of the games listed in this section, discuss the mission of the Israelite spies and how careful they would have had to be so they were not discovered. For example, while hiding in the mountains, could they have lit a campfire for cooking or warmth? No! That would have given their location away! Do you think you would have liked being picked by Joshua for such a mission? Why or why not? Then discuss this from Rahab's standpoint. How was she putting her life on the line for these men? Would the king of Jericho have considered her actions to be treason? What might he have done to her (or her family) if her actions had been discovered? It took great faith and courage for her to do the right thing when it could have been very dangerous for her to do so.

 "Digging Deeper": Research

- Rahab in the lineage of Christ – Rahab gave shelter to the Israelite spies, and as a result, she and her family were spared in the destruction of Jericho, but that is not the end of her story. Rahab married an Israelite and is listed in the genealogy of Christ. Read Matthew 1:5-6 and answer the following questions: 1) Who did Rahab marry? 2) To which tribe of Israel did her husband belong? (See verse 3) 3) What was the name of their son? 4) Who did their son marry? 5) What famous king of Israel was the great-great-grandson of Rahab? (Answers are provided in the Answer Key.)

- Sihon & Og – When Rahab told the spies that everyone in the land of Canaan was terrified of the Israelites because of what their God had done for them, the defeat of these two Amorite kings was mentioned. Read about their encounters with Israel in Numbers 21:21-35, then read Deuteronomy 3:11 to learn more about king Og.

- Flax – Rahab had stalks of flax drying on her rooftop which she used to cover and hide the Israelite spies. Use a Bible dictionary or other resource to learn more about this interesting plant and its importance in Bible times. What color flowers does the plant produce? What are its fibers used to manufacture? What ancient country was well-known for its growth and use of flax? How was it processed? Using a concordance, how many references in the Bible can you find that mention flax?

🍞 "Food For Thought": Puzzles

- Who Said It? - Read the following quotations, then choose the correct answer from the box as to who said it, and write it on the line. Some answers will be used more than once. Answers are provided in the Answer Key.

Joshua	Two spies	Jericho citizens	King of Jericho	Rahab

1. "As soon as we heard these things, our hearts melted; neither did there remain any more courage in anyone because of you, for the Lord your God, He is God in heaven above and on earth beneath." _____

2. "Truly the Lord has delivered all the land into our hands, for indeed all the inhabitants of the country are fainthearted because of us." _____

3. "Go, view the land, especially Jericho." _____

4. "Our lives for yours, if none of you tell this business of ours." _____

5. "I know that the Lord has given you the land, that the terror of you has fallen on us, and that all the inhabitants of the land are fainthearted because of you."

   _____

6. "Bring out the men who have come to you, who have entered your house, for they have come to search out all the country." _____

7. "I beg you, swear to me by the Lord, since I have shown you kindness, that you also will show kindness to my father's house, and give me a true token."

   _____

8. "It shall be, when the Lord has given us the land, that we will deal kindly and truly with you." _____

9. "Behold, men have come here tonight from the children of Israel to search out the country." _____

10. "According to your words, so be it." _____

• True or False – Read the following statements and decide if they are true or false. Write the answer on the line. Answers are provided in the Answer Key.

_____ 1. Rahab told the Israelite spies to hide in the mountains for three days before going home.

_____ 2. Rahab had stalks of flax laying on her roof.

_____ 3. Rahab let the spies down through her window with a scarlet cord.

_____ 4. Joshua sent out two spies from Acacia Grove.

_____ 5. Rahab hid the spies in a closet in her house.

_____ 6. The two spies reported back to the elders of Israel.

_____ 7. Rahab tied the scarlet cord in her window immediately after the spies left her house.

_____ 8. The spies promised Rahab that she alone would be spared when Jericho was destroyed.

_____ 9. Rahab lied to the king of Jericho in order to protect the Israelite spies.

_____ 10. Rahab and the citizens of Jericho had heard how the Lord parted the Red Sea so the Israelites could cross on dry land after leaving Egypt.

"Fruits Of Our Labor": Crafts

• Flower Pressing & Herb Drying – In our lesson, Rahab was drying stalks of flax on her rooftop. Herbs, flowers, and other plants can still be dried and preserved today and used for many things. Try your hand at one of these techniques: 1) Flower pressing: Pick flowers on a sunny day and make sure they are dry (no rain or dew on them). Lay flowers carefully on sheets of parchment paper, spreading them out so they don't overlap or touch. Cover with more parchment paper, then carefully place them between the pages of an old heavy book such as a telephone book or old dictionary. Close the book and place several heavy books on top of it to weigh it down. Now comes the patience part! Leave the flowers alone for a few weeks, no peeking! Open the book and use tweezers to carefully remove the flattened, dried flowers. Note: The flowers that work best are ones such as pansies that are not bulky. If you want to try to press a flower such as a rose, you will need to carefully slice it in half to help it "flatten" and dry properly. Once your flowers are dry, you can use them in all sorts of beautiful projects such as cards, bookmarks, candles, sun-catchers, and even framing them for display. 2) Herb drying – Drying herbs can also take patience but is very easy to do, and it's cool to be able to use them in cooking! Cut and bunch a few clean, dry stalks together (4-6), turn them upside down and secure them at the top with a rubber band or twine. Hang small bunches of herbs in a warm room out of direct sunlight and let them dry completely. This may take a few weeks. When they are completely dried, carefully slide the dried leaves into a plastic baggie or clean class jar. Discard stalks. Seal tightly, label, and store in a cool, dry place.

- Weaving - For this craft you will need a square weaving loom, a metal hook, and a bag of cotton weaving loops. These can be purchased online or at local craft stores. Weave a potholder according to the loom's directions that can be used in your kitchen. Be sure to use scarlet or red weaving loops as much as possible in your design to remind you of Rahab's faith as she served God by serving His people.

Lesson 4: Deborah & Jael
Women of Leadership & Courage

Text: Judges 4

"Growing In The Word": Lesson Text & Discussion

Read Judges 4:1-3. The nation of Israel had been involved in a pattern of being faithful to God for a little while then turning away from Him to idolatry, then being oppressed by an enemy, calling out to God for help, then being provided a deliverer from the Lord in the form of a judge. At the beginning of this chapter, Israel has once again abandoned the Lord God and turned to idolatry with all of its evil practices. Who did the Lord allow to enslave His people this time? (Jabin, king of Canaan) Who was the commander of his army? (Sisera) Israel suffered greatly under King Jabin. The Bible says he treated them harshly. He was also a very mighty king. We know this because he had 900 chariots of iron at his disposal. The Israelites would most likely have been greatly afraid of a king like this who could use such a show of force against them. How long had Jabin oppressed the people of Israel? (20 years) Once again, the Israelites cried out to God for salvation.

Read Judges 4:4-5. Israel had their 4th judge ruling over them at this time. Out of the 15 judges of Israel, all of them were men except this one. What was her name? (Deborah) We learn a couple of things about her from these verses. We know she was married and her husband's name was Lapidoth. She is also referred to as a prophetess. What do you think a prophetess is? A prophetess is simply a female version of a prophet. She would speak messages from the Lord to the people. Deborah also had a "judgment seat." That is, she was stationed between two cities, Ramah and Bethel, where the people of Israel could come to her for judgment on their problems or spiritual matters. Where did she sit? (Under a palm tree)

Read Judges 4:6-10. Israel was ready to be free from the cruel King Jabin, and God willed that they should now fight against their enemy. Deborah called a man from the tribe of Naphtali to be the commander of the army of Israel. What was his name? (Barak) Deborah, being a prophetess, knew the place God had chosen for the battle to take place and she knew who and how many should go to battle. 10,000 men from two tribes of Israel were called to fight. Which two tribes were they? (Naphtali and Zebulun) Barak received an assurance from Deborah that he would be victorious in this battle and that Sisera (Jabin's commander) would be delivered into his hand. What a wonderful message! Wouldn't you think Barak would be raring to go knowing he will be victorious in battle before he even goes out to fight? You might think so, but he wasn't. He wanted an extra assurance. He wanted Deborah to go with him. Did she agree? (Yes) Deborah also told Barak that because of this, he would not receive any glory from the day. Their enemy, Sisera, would be delivered into the hand of a woman. Now before we're too hard on Barak and think he's being cowardly, let's look at **Hebrews 11:32-34**. Barak is listed in this great faith chapter. He did go to battle and was victorious and this was credited to him because he was a man of faith.

Read Judges 4:11. This verse may seem a little out of place as we wonder what it has to do with anything, but it is giving us a piece of information that will mean more later on. A man named Heber lived near Kedesh, a city of the tribe of Naphtali. What did he live in? (A tent) File this away in your mind, and we'll come back to it later on in the chapter.

Read Judges 4:12-16. Let the battle begin! Sisera probably felt pretty confident as he gathered his 900 chariots and the rest of his army to go against 10,000 Israelites. Meanwhile, Deborah gave Barak the word from the Lord that it was time to engage in battle. Who went before Barak, destroying Jabin's army? (The Lord) This is why the Israelites were victorious. When the Lord is on your side and fighting for you, *no one* will defeat you. As the Canaanite army was being heavily defeated, Sisera hopped down from his chariot and ran away to try to save his own life. How successful was Barak against Sisera's army? (He killed all of them. Not a man was left.)

Read Judges 4:17. While all of his army was dead, Sisera was still alive and running for his life. He escaped to the tent of Jael, the wife of Heber the Kenite. Remember, this was the man we read about in verse 11. Sisera felt safe here because Heber and King Jabin were at peace with each other. They were not enemies, so Sisera did not think he had anything to fear.

Read Judges 4:18-20. Jael immediately made Sisera comfortable. He was exhausted from battle and laid down. She covered him with a blanket and brought him something to drink. He had asked for water, but she brought him something else instead. What was it? (Milk) Have you ever heard of people drinking a glass of warm milk at bedtime to help themselves sleep? We're not told why she gave him milk instead of water, but it could have been for this reason. Sisera gave Jael some final instructions before he let himself doze off. He wanted her to stand guard at the door of the tent to make sure no one entered. What did he want her to do if someone asked her if a man was inside? (He wanted her to lie and say, "No.") So far, everything seemed to be working out well for Sisera. He managed to escape from a battle where his army was completely destroyed, and he made it to a tent of a friend where he could be safe. His worries were over, right? Watch what Jael does next.

Read Judges 4:21-24. Sisera was exhausted and fell fast asleep. Jael tiptoed up to him with two things in her hands. What were they? (A hammer and a tent peg) She placed the tent peg at his temple and drove it through his head and into the ground with her hammer.

The enemy of the Israelites was dead by the hands of a woman, just as Deborah had said. Barak had been pursuing Sisera and was hot on his trail. He stopped by the tent and Jael invited him inside, knowing who he was looking for. Barak went in and saw Sisera dead. God gave a great victory to His people that day and great salvation and relief to them from their oppressor. Deborah continued to serve as the judge of Israel for forty years.

These two women of the Bible showed great courage and leadership to help God's people in a desperate time of need.

Review Questions: (Answers are provided in the Answer Key.)

1. What number judge was Deborah out of the 15 judges of Israel?

2. What are three things we know about Deborah?

3. How long had King Jabin been oppressing Israel?

4. What was the name of Jabin's general?

5. What was the name of Deborah's general?

6. How many men of Israel were called to battle?

7. What two tribes of Israel did these soldiers come from?

8. How many chariots of iron did King Jabin have?

9. Who was Heber the Kenite's wife?

10. Which army was successful in the battle, the Israelites or the Canaanites, and why?

11. Where did Sisera escape to?

12. What did Jael give him to drink?

13. What did Sisera do next?

14. What happened to him at this time?

15. Who arrived at Heber's tent and found out what had happened?

"Putting Down Roots": Memory Work

- Memorize Psalm 20:7

- Memorize Judges 4:4-5

- Memorize the 15 judges of Israel: Othniel, Ehud, Shamgar, Deborah, Gideon, Abimelech, Tola, Jair, Jephthah, Ibzan, Elon, Abdon, Samson, Eli, Samuel

 ## "Farther Afield": Map Work

Map 4

- Locate the city of Harosheth Hagoyim

- Locate the city of Ramah

- Locate the city of Bethel

- Locate the city of Kedesh

- Locate the Kishon River

- Locate Mt. Tabor

- Locate the city of Zaanaim

 ## "Harvest Fun": Games & Activities

- Which Woman? - This activity is for 2 players or 2 teams. For this activity, you will need to think fast to remember which fact card describes which woman, Deborah or Jael. To prepare, each player or team needs 2 name cards. One card will have the name of "Deborah" and the other "Jael." Place the players' or teams' name cards on a table at one end of the room. Have someone prepare the fact cards ahead of time, writing one fact per card and making two sets of identical fact cards. Each player or team will have their own set of twelve fact cards. To get ready to play, place a stack of fact cards at the opposite end of the room from the name cards. When "Go" is called, let each player (or one member per team) race with one fact card to the other end of the room, placing it in the column under the correct name. Fact cards must be taken one at a time. The first player or team to place all of their fact cards ends the game. A scorekeeper may then check the fact cards, awarding one point for each fact card correctly placed. The player or team with the most points wins. (You may also do this activity just as a review without racing or keeping score.)

Deborah facts: 1) Spent time between Ramah and Bethel, 2) Prophetess, 3) Wife of Lapidoth, 4) Judge of Israel, 5) Sat under a palm tree, 6) Went to battle with Barak

Jael facts: 1) Killed Sisera, 2) Wife of Heber, 3) Handy with a hammer,4) Served milk, 5) Gave Barak good news, 6) Husband was a Kenite

- Sword Drills – In this lesson, battles were fought with chariots and real swords. We have swords too, that are more powerful than anything fashioned out of metal! Ephesians 6:17 tells us that we have the "*sword of the Spirit, which is the word of God.*" A good soldier practices using his sword so it is very familiar to him and he is comfortable using it. Let's practice using our swords with some sword drills. Each person needs to have a Bible. As the following scripture references are called out, everyone will try to locate the verse as quickly as possible. The first person to find it will read it aloud once everyone has had time to turn to it, or you may simply take turns reading aloud. The point is not to win a race but to get familiar with our Bibles so we can use them effectively. These twenty verses are all about strength and courage: Joshua 1:9; Isaiah 41:10; Ephesians 6:10; Psalm 27:1; Hebrews 13:5-6; Zephaniah 3:17; Philippians 4:13; Revelation 2:10; Proverbs 28:1; Deuteronomy 31:6; John 14:27; II Timothy 1:7; Psalm 56:3-4; I Chronicles 28:20; Job 5:11; I John 4:18; Exodus 14:13; Matthew 10:28; I Corinthians 16:13; I Samuel 30:6.

"Digging Deeper": Research

- The Song of Deborah – Judges chapter 5 is a song of Deborah and Barak which they sang after the victory recorded in chapter 4. Read the song and answer the following questions regarding it: 1) Who is praised in verse 2? 2) How did the earth, clouds, and mountains respond when the Lord marched forth? 3) How is Deborah described in verse 7? 4) According to verse 15, which tribe of Israel was strongly with Deborah and which one wanted to be but never acted on it? 5) According to verse 16, which two tribes stayed in ships or by the seashore? 6) Which two tribes of Israel jeopardized their lives on the battlefield according to verse 18? 7) Who is praised and given a tribute in verses 24-27? 8) According to verse 28, who was anxiously waiting at a window, watching for someone to come back home? 9) To what do Deborah and Barak compare those who love the Lord in verse 31? 10) At the conclusion of the song, we are told how many years the Israelites had rest and peace under Deborah's leadership. How many years was it? (Answers are provided in the Answer Key.)

- Deborah the Prophetess – A prophetess in the Bible would do the same job as a prophet, the only difference being she was a woman. Deborah would have been a messenger of the Lord to His people, or a spokeswoman for God. She is not the only woman mentioned in scripture with this title. Research and list all of the women (named and unnamed) in scripture who were called a prophetess or who were said to have prophesied. Write down any descriptions or facts about each one as well.

 # "Food For Thought": Puzzles

- The following page contains a crossword puzzle for this lesson. Answers are provided in the Answer Key.

Across

3 Barak led his troops from Mt. _____

7 King Jabin had 900 of these

8 Deborah's husband

9 Deborah sat between Ramah and _____

11 The general of King Jabin's army

12 Moses father-in-law

13 What Jael gave Sisera to drink

14 Jael's husband

Down

1 Type of tree Deborah sat under

2 Deborah was the _____ judge of Israel

4 Sisera entered Heber's _____

5 Jabin was king of this nation

6 Besides a judge, Deborah was also this

9 The Israelite general

10 Jael used this to drive a tent peg

- Matching – Match the name of the person on the left with his or her correct description on the right. Answers are provided in the Answer Key.

_____ 1. Hobab   a. husband of Deborah

_____ 2. Deborah   b. Moses' father-in-law

_____ 3. Lapidoth   c. King of Canaan

_____ 4. Barak   d. the Kenite

_____ 5. Heber   e. commander of Canaanite army

_____ 6. Jabin   f. wife of Heber

_____ 7. Ehud   g. father of Barak

_____ 8. Sisera   h. prophetess

_____ 9. Jael   i. 2nd judge of Israel

_____10. Abinoam   j. commander of Israelite army

"Fruits Of Our Labor": Crafts

- Clay Sculpting – Make a sculpture of Deborah sitting under the palm tree. Sculpey clay is fun to use and can be baked to harden and preserve your sculpture. To avoid using too much costly clay, use crumpled up aluminum foil as a "base" for the trunk of the tree and for Deborah's body, then mold clay around the foil and sculpt as you'd like. Bake at 275 degrees for 15 minutes for every $\frac{1}{4}$ inch thickness of clay. Let cool completely before handling. Sculpey clay comes in a variety of colors and can be found at your local craft store. It can also be painted after it is baked and dried.

- Diorama - A diorama is a scene in miniature. It can be made in a shoebox, or on a wooden base. To create the scene you can use just about any kind of materials such as action figures, clay, styrofoam, paper, aluminum foil, Lego blocks, paint, stickers, etc. To get ideas for some cool effects for water, fire, grass and other features, check out some books from the library on dioramas or go online (with permission) and look at some tutorials. Make a diorama of one of the scenes from this lesson. If you made the clay sculpture of Deborah sitting under the palm tree, you could include that in a diorama. You could also choose one of the battle scenes or the scene of Sisera sleeping in the tent of Jael. Be creative and have fun with this! *Tip – When making a diorama with a lot of people, such as a battle scene, it is helpful to find an old Risk game at a yard sale or thrift store. There are lots of tiny plastic men that work really well in a diorama such as this.

© 2018, Pryor Convictions Media, Paul & Heather Pryor, St. Petersburg, FL

Lesson 5: Hannah

A Woman of Prayer

Text: I Samuel 1; 2:18-21

"Growing In The Word": Lesson Text & Discussion

Read I Samuel 1:1-2. This lesson takes place during the period of the judges. Before the Israelites ever had a king, they were ruled by a judge. We studied about one of them, Deborah, in our last lesson. There were 15 judges in all, and at this time, Eli the 14th judge is the spiritual leader of Israel. In these verses, we are introduced to a man named Elkanah. What tribe of Israel was he from? (Ephraim) He had two wives. What were their names? (Peninnah and Hannah) From the very beginning of time, God's plan for marriage has been one man for one woman, but we see many examples in the Old Testament of polygamy, which is having more than one wife. Any time man tries to change God's plan, it doesn't turn out well and many problems arise. As we will see as we read on, all is not well in Elkanah's family. There was a big difference between these two wives of Elkanah. What was it? (Peninnah had children, but Hannah did not.)

Read I Samuel 1:3-5. Elkanah would travel to Shiloh once each year to worship the Lord and offer sacrifices. Shiloh was the city where the tabernacle was located. The tabernacle was a huge tent which served as the center of worship for the Jews at this time. The priests would work there daily and offer sacrifices. Eli served as high priest (as well as judge), and his two sons served as priests under him. What were the names of his sons? (Hophni and Phinehas) This particular offering which Elkanah made was divided up. Part of it was offered to the Lord while the remainder was for he and his family to eat. He made sure that Peninnah and her children had some to eat, but what did he do special for Hannah? (He gave her a double portion.) Why did he do this? (Because he loved her) In ancient times, it was a very big deal to be childless. Women who were in that situation were often looked down on, but Elkanah loved Hannah even more than his other wife who had borne him several children. He felt a particular tenderness for Hannah and treated her very well. She was clearly "the favorite wife," and that didn't sit well with Peninnah at all.

Read I Samuel 1:6-8. Peninnah is referred to as Hannah's "rival" or "adversary." Do you know what those words mean? They mean an enemy, or someone who is against you. So, did these two wives of Elkanah get along well? (Not at all!) Not only did Peninnah not like Hannah, she provoked or picked on her severely. She delighted in making Hannah miserable.

She taunted her constantly with the fact that she (Peninnah) had children while Hannah did not. This would have been completely devastating to Hannah. It was heartbreaking enough to not have any children of her own, but to have it rubbed in her face, day after day, and be made fun of for it and cruelly tormented about it would have been almost more than she could bear. How did Hannah react to all of the torment from Peninnah? (She wept.) Wouldn't you? This constant torment from her rival, and daily reminders of what she did not have made her so sad. It even reached the point that Hannah could not eat the generous portion her husband gave to her at the yearly sacrifice. Did her husband notice this? (Yes) He noticed, but he didn't necessarily understand. He knew Hannah couldn't have any children, but he thought because he loved her so much, she shouldn't be sad about what she *didn't* have but should be happy about what she *did* have. He even asked her, *"Am I not better to you than ten sons?"*

Read I Samuel 1:9-11. How is Hannah described as feeling at this time? (She was in anguish and bitterness of soul.) She had reached the end of her rope. She was so sad and hurt, so she did the best thing she could possibly do. What was it? (She prayed to God.) She went to the tabernacle and poured out her heart in prayer to God. Prayer is powerful. Not only do we pray for things we would like God to do for us or ways to help us, we also pray to tell God how we feel. When we are sad or hurt, angry, or even happy, God wants us to talk to Him about it. He loves us, and He cares about how we feel. As Hannah prayed to God, she made a vow. A vow is a promise. What did she promise God? (She promised the Lord that if He would give her a son, she would give him back to God to be in service to Him all of his life.) Wow! Can you imagine making such a promise? Hannah wants a child so very badly, yet she is willing to give him back to God to serve Him. What unusual thing did she say about the child's hair? (She told the Lord that no razor would ever touch his head. He would never get a haircut!) It may seem strange that Hannah was never going to cut the child's hair, but what she is doing is promising the Lord that the child would be a Nazirite. A Nazirite was someone who was set apart for special service to God either for a certain period of time in their life or for their entire life. There were certain rules a Nazirite had to follow, one of them being that a razor would not touch his head. (You can learn more about the interesting life of a Nazirite in the research portion of this lesson.)

Read I Samuel 1:12-18. While Hannah was praying, someone was watching. Who was sitting at the door of the tabernacle? (Eli) What did he think of Hannah and why? (He thought she was drunk because he only saw her lips moving but could not hear her praying. She was praying silently.) He fusses at her for being intoxicated (drunk) and tells her to straighten up! How did Hannah respond to him? (She denied being drunk and explained how sorrowful she was and that she was pouring her heart out to the Lord.) Eli realized he was mistaken about Hannah and gives her a blessing. What did Eli tell her to do? (He told her to go in peace, and that God would grant her petition.) Eli set Hannah's heart at ease. He realized she had asked something of the Lord, and he told her that God would answer her prayer. She was finally able to have peace in her heart because she knew God had listened and would act. She didn't have to be sad or anxious anymore. **Philippians 4:6-7** tells us to *"Be anxious for nothing but in everything by prayer and supplication with thanksgiving, let your requests be made known unto God and the peace of God which passes all understanding will guard your hearts and minds in Christ Jesus."* This is exactly what Hannah did. She was anxious and sad so she poured out her heart to God and made her request ("Please give me a son!"). After doing that, she was able to have peace and go on her way, no longer sad.

Read I Samuel 1:19-20. What did Hannah, Elkanah, and the rest of them do the next day? (They worshiped the Lord and returned home.) Verse 19 says that the Lord remembered her. This doesn't mean that he had forgotten all about Hannah, and then suddenly remembered her again. Whenever the Bible says that the Lord remembers someone, it means He is about to act. Hannah had the son she had prayed for and wanted for such a long time. What did she name him? (Samuel) What does the name Samuel mean? (It means "asked of the Lord.")

Read I Samuel 1:21-23. Hannah had her precious baby at last, but the yearly feast at Shiloh rolled around again. Why did Hannah stay home? Hannah had not forgotten her vow she made to the Lord. She had promised to give the child back to God to be in His service for life, but she needed to wait until the child was weaned. That means until he was old enough that he could eat solid food on his own and no longer be nursed by his mother. She was determined that she would not appear before the Lord at the tabernacle until Samuel was old enough that she could present him to God as she had promised, to remain at the tabernacle for service. For the Jewish woman in Bible times, a child was usually weaned at two or three years of age. Did Elkanah agree to this? (Yes) This is really amazing. Samuel is Elkanah's son too. Hannah had vowed in her prayer to the Lord to give Samuel back to God, but Elkanah had not promised any such thing. **Numbers 30:6-8** even says that if a husband does not agree to a vow that his wife made to the Lord, he can overrule it, and the Lord will forgive the woman for breaking the vow, but we do not see that here. Elkanah realizes the seriousness of making a vow to the Lord, and that one should pay what one promises. (Numbers 30:2; Deuteronomy 23:21-23) He agrees with Hannah in all of this and is satisfied and at peace with what she will do.

Read I Samuel 1:24-28. Now comes the hard part. Samuel has been weaned and is old enough to be presented to the Lord at the tabernacle. Hannah must take her little son to Shiloh and leave him there forever as she had promised the Lord she would do. Not only did she prepare to take Samuel, she also took items to be offered to the Lord. When they arrived in Shiloh, whom did she take Samuel to? (She took him to Eli, the high priest.) It had been a few years since Eli had last seen Hannah and spoken to her, so she reminds him of who she is.

She also told Eli about the promise she made to God concerning little Samuel. The Bible doesn't say how old Samuel is at this time, but how is he described? (He is described as being young.) Hannah praised God before Eli, describing how she had prayed for that child, and how God had answered her. She then told Eli that Samuel was to be devoted to serving God the rest of his life, then she left her precious little son in Eli's care. Instead of being sorrowful, Hannah and her family worshiped God. Hannah was so thankful that God had blessed her with a son, and she was happy for him to grow up serving the great God who answers prayer.

Read I Samuel 2:18-21. Leaving Samuel in Shiloh with Eli was not the last time Hannah ever saw her son. Each year, she and her husband continued to travel to Shiloh for the annual feast, and she would visit her child. As Samuel ministered before the Lord, what would he wear? (A linen ephod) This was a type of long shirt or tunic that the priests were required to wear. Hannah always brought a gift for her little son. What would she lovingly make and give to him each year? (A little robe) Eli would pray a special blessing on Hannah and her husband each year when they came to Shiloh. What was it? (He prayed that the Lord would bless them with more children to reward Hannah for giving Samuel in service to the Lord.) God answered this prayer as well. How many other children did Hannah and Elkanah have? (They had three sons and two daughters.) We know that Hannah was a loving mother and a faithful follower of God. She had taught her little son well as we see that he was very dedicated to God as he grew. **Read I Samuel 2:26.**

Hannah teaches us about the value and power of prayer. She shows us what to do when we are sad and hurt, and she shows how to have peace after leaving our cares and requests with the Lord.

Review Questions: (Answers are provided in the Answer Key.)

1. Which tribe of Israel did Elkanah belong to?

2. What is polygamy?

3. Who were Eli's two sons?

4. What was the Jewish center of worship which was located in Shiloh?

5. At the yearly sacrifice in Shiloh, what did Elkanah give to Hannah?

6. Describe Peninnah's treatment of Hannah.

7. Why did Elkanah think Hannah should not be upset?

8. When Hannah was in anguish and "bitterness of soul", what did she do?

9. What promise did Hannah make to the Lord?

10. What was a Nazirite?

11. What did Eli think of Hannah when she was at the door of the tabernacle, and why did he think this?

12. What did Eli tell Hannah after she explained to him about her prayer to God?

13. How did Hannah leave Shiloh?

14. What scripture in the New Testament tells us not to be anxious and how to have peace in our hearts?

15. What does it mean in the Bible whenever it says the Lord remembers someone?

16. What does Samuel's name mean?

17. Why did Hannah not go to Shiloh after Samuel was born?

18. Did Elkanah agree or disagree with Hannah's vow?

19. Could Elkanah have canceled Hannah's vow if he had wanted to?

20. In whose care did Hannah leave Samuel as he grew and served the Lord?

21. How often did Hannah see Samuel after leaving him in Shiloh?

22. What did she bring him at each visit?

23. What blessing did Eli pray for Elkanah and Hannah each time they visited Shiloh?

24. How many other children did the Lord bless Hannah with?

25. Write I Samuel 2:26.

"Putting Down Roots": Memory Work

- Memorize I Samuel 1:27

- Memorize Philippians 4:6-7

- Memorize I Peter 5:7

 ## "Farther Afield": Map Work
Map 4

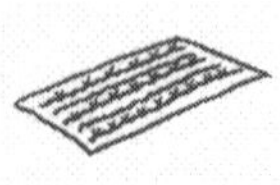

- Locate the city of Ramathaim Zophim

- Locate the city of Shiloh

- Locate the city of Ramah

 ## "Harvest Fun": Games & Activities

- Who/What Am I? - For this game, you will simply need a few index cards or pieces of paper. Have someone who is not playing the game, write the name of a person or a thing, one per card, from this lesson. (Suggested list follows.) Tape a card to the back of each participant so they cannot see who or what they are. Let all the participants look at each other's cards. Then, pair off participants, letting them take turns asking yes or no questions of their partner to try to guess who or what they are. For example, one player has a card which reads "tabernacle" on his back while his partner has a card which reads "Peninnah" on her back. The "tabernacle" may ask "Peninnah", "Am I a person?" She would respond, "No." Then it would be her turn to ask a question. She might ask the "tabernacle," "Am I married?" He would answer, "Yes." Play would continue until one of them guesses correctly. After the first round, remove the cards off of everyone's backs, shuffle them up, and give new ones to the winners of the first round. All other players are out. Play continues for another round. If you'd like, this game can go on until one player is left. The following words are a suggested list for the cards, but you can make up as many others as you'd like as long as they come from this lesson. Card words: tabernacle, Peninnah, Eli, sacrifice, Hannah, prayer, baby, priest, razor, wine, bull, robe, Samuel, husband, Shiloh, heart.

- Prayer Journal - I Thessalonians 5:17 tells us to "pray without ceasing." There are so many people who need us to pray for them, and we need to be persistent in "asking, seeking, and knocking." We can pray for those who are sick, those who are sad, those in leadership both of the church and our nation, missionaries, soldiers... Like Hannah, we also have our own needs and desires that we should be diligently praying for. Start a prayer journal where you can write down what you want to pray for and the date of the prayer request or date that you first started praying for it. Write down any answers you see to your prayers such as someone getting well or finding a job. It is so encouraging to look back through your prayer journal after several months and see how God has answered different prayers. (Instructions to make your own prayer journal are in the crafts section of this lesson, or you can purchase a blank journal from a store.)

 ## "Digging Deeper": Research

- The Tabernacle – The tabernacle was the center of worship for the Jews from the time of Moses until King Solomon built the first temple during the time of the United Kingdom. This is where Hannah and her husband came yearly to offer sacrifices and where Samuel grew up and served the Lord. Research images of what the tabernacle and its furniture might have looked like as well as the placement of the different furnishings. Read Exodus 36, 37, 38 and 40 for a detailed description of the tabernacle, its furnishings, and how everything was to be set up. After you research it, try drawing or building a model to scale of what this place of worship looked like.

- Nazarite Vow – Read Numbers 6 for rules regarding a Nazirite vow. Were men the only ones allowed to be Nazirites? Was a Nazirite vow for life or could it be for a short period of time? What were some things Nazirites were not allowed to do? Can you find any other examples in the Bible besides Samuel of someone who was a Nazirite?

- Hannah's Prayer – I Samuel 2:1-10 records a prayer of Hannah. Read her prayer then answer the following questions: 1) According to verse 1, what was Hannah able to do to her enemies? 2) Who might have been considered an enemy(s) of Hannah? 3) What does she compare God to in verse 2? 4) According to verse 3, what are the proud and arrogant warned of? 5) What are the five contrasting things the Lord does that are listed in verses 6-8? 6) According to verse 9, what does the Lord guard? 7) In verse 10, who will be broken in pieces?

 **"Food For Thought": Puzzles**

- Coded Message – Use the Key to break the code.

__ __ __ __ __ __   __ __ __ __ __ __ __   __ __ __
19 26 13 13 26 19   19 12 13 12 9 22 23   19 22 9

__ __ __   __ __   __ __ __   __ __ __ __.
5 12 4   7 12   7 19 22   15 12 6 23

Key to the Code:

F	N	R	U	A	G	O	S	V	C	H	T	D	I	E	B	W	K	Y	P	M	L	J
21	13	9	6	26	20	12	8	5	24	19	7	23	18	22	25	4	16	2	11	14	15	17

- Before or After? - In I Samuel 1:17, Eli made an important statement to Hannah when he told her, "*Go in peace, and the God of Israel grant your petition which you have asked of Him.*" Hannah's life was very different before and after Eli said this to her. Read the following statements from the lesson and decide if they happened before or after Eli said this. Write the correct answer on the line. Answers are provided in the Answer Key.

_____ 1. And Elkanah knew Hannah his wife and the Lord remembered her.

_____ 2. Hannah said, "*As your soul lives, my lord, I am the woman who stood by you here, praying to the Lord.*"

_____ 3. Elkanah asked Hannah if he was not better to her than 10 sons.

_____ 4. Hannah made a vow to the Lord.

_____ 5. Hannah went on her way, and her face was no longer sad.

_____ 6. Peninnah provoked Hannah severely.

_____ 7. Elkanah gave Hannah double portions of the offering.

_____ 8. Hannah did not go up to Shiloh with her husband for the yearly offering.

_____ 9. Hannah said, "*For this child I prayed, and the Lord has granted me my petition which I asked of Him.*"

_____ 10. Eli thought Hannah was drunk.

"Fruits Of Our Labor": Crafts

- Sew a Coat – Hannah lovingly made a little coat for Samuel every year. Use the coat template in Appendix B for this craft. Copy the template onto card stock. Color or paint to decorate if desired. Hole punch at the places indicated. Thread a large plastic "needle" with a yarn color of your choice. Start at one hole bringing the needle up from the bottom and bringing the yarn almost all of the way through. Leave a small tail of yarn and tape it securely to the back of the coat.

Now begin whip-stitching the yarn all the way around the edges of the coat. To whip stitch, simply take your needle that has been brought up through the first hole, circle around the edge and bring the needle back up from underneath through the second hole. Pull straight up until somewhat tight, then repeat by circling around the edge and back up through the back at the third hole. Continue sewing the coat until the last hole is reached. Bring the needle down through it, clip the yarn leaving a 1 inch tail, and secure it to the back with tape.

- Prayer Journal - To make your own prayer journal, you will need two pieces of craft foam (same size), several sheets of lined or plain paper, a hole puncher, and yarn. First, cut or fold the paper to the size you want your journal to be. Next, cut the foam pieces about 1/2" larger than the paper. These will be the front and back covers of your journal. Use the hole puncher to punch three holes in the foam pieces and the paper. You need a hole near the top, a hole in the middle and one near the bottom. Each hole needs to be about 1/4" in from the edge. Assemble the journal by placing the paper inside the covers and lining up the holes. Use three pieces of yarn to tie the book together at each hole. Decorate the front of the journal any way you wish. You can use markers or foam letter stickers to spell out "Prayer Journal." Be as creative as you'd like with the cover. You may even want to write some scriptures about prayer on the cover or the first page such as I Thessalonians 5:17, James 5:16 or Mark 11:24.

Lesson 6: The Queen of Sheba
A Woman Seeking Wisdom

Text: I Kings 10:1-13

"Growing In The Word": Lesson Text & Discussion

Read I Kings 10:1. After Jesus, Solomon was the wisest man who ever lived. When he became king of Israel, the Lord was pleased with him and asked him what He could give him. Solomon asked for wisdom to rule God's people well, and the Lord blessed him with it. His wisdom was so amazing, that people all over the world heard about it. He was famous for it. Now, you might be asking yourself, "What exactly is wisdom?" Some people think wisdom means knowledge. It is true that when you are wise, you have knowledge, but you can have knowledge and not be wise. For instance, you might know that God says to obey your parents, but if you choose to disobey them, you are not wise. Wisdom is the ability to make right decisions and use good judgment. It uses knowledge in the right way. The queen of Sheba had heard all about the wisdom of king Solomon, and she was very curious. She had a lot of questions she wanted answered and who better to do that than the wisest person on earth? She decided to pay Solomon a visit to test his wisdom and knowledge. She traveled from the South to visit the city of Jerusalem in the country of Israel. We don't exactly where she came from, but two possibilities are the country of Ethiopia or the country of Arabia. In Matthew 12:42 and Luke 11:31, Jesus refers to her as "the queen of the South" and praises her for traveling so far to seek wisdom.

Read I Kings 10:2-3. When she arrived in the city of Jerusalem, people probably stopped on the streets and stared. She came with a very large company of servants, animals, and gifts for the king. Numerous camels were loaded down with these precious gifts. What were they? (Spices, gold, and precious gemstones) The queen of Sheba didn't waste any time in speaking to Solomon. There were so many questions she was anxious to ask him. Did she ask him all of the questions she had, or did she keep some to herself? (She asked him everything that was in her heart.) How many of her questions was Solomon able to answer? (He answered all of them.) There was no question or subject that was too hard for Solomon to answer or explain. This was not because he was a genius of some sort, but remember that God had given him the gift of wisdom.

Read I Kings 10:4-5. Not only did the queen of Sheba hear the wisdom of Solomon when she talked to him, she saw his wisdom demonstrated in many ways as he took her on a guided tour of his house. What were some of the things she saw that impressed her? (Solomon's house that he had built, the food that was served in it, his servants and their clothing, the drinking vessels that the cup-bearers held, and the entryway to the temple from his house) Solomon may have treated the visiting queen to a banquet at which she saw many of these things, or he may have walked her through a room while some people in his house were dining, and she was able to see these things. Either way, she saw them and was completely overwhelmed with it all. How does the Bible describe the effect on her? ("There was no more spirit in her.") Not only did the queen of Sheba hear the wisdom of Solomon, she saw it in all that he showed her. You might wonder how she was able to "see" wisdom. Remember that wisdom is the ability to make right decisions and show good judgment. It uses knowledge in the best way. The queen could see that Solomon had good taste and showed good judgment in running his house well. His servants were well-dressed and ate good food. Why would it be wise for a king to dress his servants richly and feed them well? (Servants who are treated well will usually be faithful and dedicated to their master, doing their work well.) Solomon's wealth showed in his beautifully built and decorated house, yet wisdom would show in how he designed things to be functional but still beautiful.

Read I Kings 10:6-10. After talking with Solomon and taking the tour, she admitted that everything she had heard about him was true. But did she believe it before visiting him? (No) The reports just seemed so incredible, so impossible. She just couldn't believe that he could be as wise and as wealthy as everyone said, but after seeing everything with her own eyes, she was a believer! Had she been given an accurate report about Solomon in her own land, or was there more to the story? (More! She said she had not been told the half about his wisdom and wealth.) How did she describe his servants? (Happy) She felt that all of Solomon's servants were blessed to be working for such a king as he. They were blessed to be treated so well, and blessed to be able to be around him continually, hearing his great wisdom. After describing Solomon's servants as blessed, the queen acknowledges the Lord as blessed for putting Solomon on the throne to be the king of Israel. What two reasons does she give for God making Solomon king? (1-To do justice, and 2- To do righteousness) It was Solomon's job as king to carry out justice for his people. When someone wrongs us today, we have a court system that carries out justice. In Solomon's time, people would go to the king to plead their cases, and let him decide a just punishment for a wrongdoer. Solomon was also to do righteousness which means he was to live right and do right in all things. Do each of us have a responsibility to "do righteousness" before God today? (Yes!) The queen of Sheba was satisfied with her visit. She was able to hear the wisdom of Solomon for herself and see the majesty of his kingdom, given to him and blessed by the Lord God. Before she returned to her home country, she gave gifts to king Solomon. What were they? (120 talents of gold, spices and precious stones.) These were the things she had loaded on all the camels she brought with her. A talent was a measurement of weight. 120 talents of gold would be a very expensive gift. Precious stones would be very valuable as well. These would be gems such as rubies, diamonds, pearls, emeralds, etc. But spices may not seem like such a big deal. After all, we go to the grocery store and buy them for a few dollars a bottle. In ancient times, certain spices only grew in certain countries or regions, so if you wanted something particular that didn't grow where you lived, you had to buy it from a market that got it imported by ship or caravan from a far country. This would make the spice rare and much more expensive to buy. Did the queen of Sheba bring Solomon just a few spices? (No) The Bible says there was never again such an abundance of spices as she brought to Solomon.

Read I Kings 10:11-12. These two verses talk more about the additions to Solomon's wealth, and what he did with some of it. Solomon had a great navy in the Red Sea (the fleet of Hiram) which brought in goods to the kingdom of Israel. What three things did Solomon's ships import (bring) from the land of Ophir? (Gold, precious stones, almug wood) Gold and precious stones were also among the gifts given to Solomon by the queen of Sheba. What did Solomon use some of the almug wood for? (He made steps for the house of the Lord [the temple], the kings house, and for harps and stringed instruments.) Almug wood was thought to be a beautiful dark reddish wood. Try looking for pictures of it.

Read I Kings 10:13. The queen of Sheba's visit is over, and she is preparing to return to her home country. What did Solomon give her? (He gave her whatever she asked for.) He generously gave her whatever she was interested in having and taking home with her. It would be interesting to know what some of those gifts were. Maybe she wanted some things that were unique to Israel and not found in her own homeland, like certain exotic plants, insects or animals. Maybe she wanted some things to remind her of their conversations and of the great wisdom Solomon showed as he answered all of her questions. Whatever they were, the queen of Sheba leaves us an example of someone who was seeking wisdom and was willing to go to great lengths to find it.

James 1:5 tells us that if anyone needs wisdom, he should ask God, and God will give it to him. The book of Proverbs, which was written by Solomon, is full of verses that talk about how important wisdom is and how we can be wise. **Proverbs 2:6** tells us that *"the Lord gives wisdom."* Becoming wise is not always easy, but it is very important. In the New Testament, Jesus mentions the queen of Sheba and how far she traveled to seek wisdom. (Matthew 12:42, Luke 11:31) How far will you go to seek wisdom?

Review Questions: (Answers are provided in the Answer Key.)

1. What is wisdom?

2. Where was the queen of Sheba from?

3. What gifts did the queen of Sheba bring for the king?

4. How many of the queen of Sheba's questions was Solomon unable to answer?

5. After hearing the wisdom of Solomon, what did he show the queen of Sheba?

6. What was the reaction of the queen of Sheba to all of this?

7. How did Solomon show wisdom in the way he treated his servants?

8. How did the queen of Sheba describe the servants of Solomon?

9. The queen of Sheba acknowledged that the Lord made Solomon king and gave two reasons why. What were they?

10. What gifts did the queen of Sheba give to king Solomon before she returned home?

11. What three items did Solomon's navy bring from the land of Ophir?

12. What did Solomon use almug wood for?

13. What gifts did Solomon give the queen of Sheba before she returned home?

14. What Old Testament verse and what New Testament verse tell us that God gives wisdom?

15. Who wrote the book of Proverbs?

 "Putting Down Roots": Memory Work

- Memorize Proverbs 2:6

- Memorize James 1:5

"Farther Afield": Map Work

Map 1

- Locate the country of Ethiopia

- Locate the country of Arabia

  (The queen of Sheba was from a country to the south of Israel. One of these two countries was probably her homeland.)

- Locate the Red Sea

- Locate the city of Jerusalem

- Locate the land of Ophir

"Harvest Fun": Games & Activities

- Seek Wisdom #1 – The object of this game is to find wisdom. Write the word "wisdom" in large letters on one side of an index card, then write "Happy is the man who finds wisdom, and the man who gains understanding" (Proverbs 3:13) on the other side of the card. Take turns hiding the card somewhere in the house then let others seek it. The hider can give "hot and cold" clues to help others locate the wisdom card. Whoever finds it first is the winner and gets to hide it next, but first have him or her read aloud Proverbs 3:13 which is written on the card. After playing the game, talk about where we should really look for wisdom and how important it is to find it.

- "The Wisest One of All" - For this game, all players will take turns asking a question of the player on their left. The questions can be random, such as "What is 3x6?", or they can be chosen from a list of questions, or limited to just Bible review questions. If a player answers correctly, he stays in the game. If he answers incorrectly, he is out. Play continues until there is only one player left. He or she is "the wisest one of all" for answering all questions correctly. Of course, this is just for fun. There isn't anyone who could answer every question correctly that a person could ask. After playing, remind everyone that Solomon was able to correctly answer every question that the queen of Sheba asked him, then discuss how this was so.

- Seek Wisdom #2 – This activity will be practiced daily for about a month. Just as the queen of Sheba was seeking wisdom from king Solomon, we can also learn from the wisdom of Solomon by reading the book of Proverbs. Proverbs contains 31 chapters so if you read one chapter a day, it takes about a month to read the entire book. This is a good practice to do every day throughout your life in addition to your other Bible study/reading. Never stop seeking wisdom!

"Digging Deeper": Research

- Wisdom vs. Foolishness – Solomon wrote the book on wisdom (literally!) when he penned Proverbs. That book of the Bible has a lot to say about wisdom and foolishness, but there are other scriptures throughout the Bible that speak about these subjects as well. Make two columns on a piece of paper, labeling one "Wisdom" and the other "Foolishness". Read each of the following scriptures, placing each of them in the correct category of wisdom or foolishness. (Some verses will be listed in both categories.) Next to each verse, write a brief description or summary of the verse as to what wisdom or foolishness is, does, or results in. Scripture list: Psalm 111:10; Jeremiah 8:9; I Corinthians 1:20; I Corinthians 3:19; James 3:14-15; James 3:17; Proverbs 1:7; Proverbs 3:21-24; Proverbs 8:11; Proverbs 10:8; Proverbs 11:30; Proverbs 12:15; Proverbs 13:1; Proverbs 13:20; Proverbs 14:9; Proverbs 14:16; Proverbs 14:17; Proverbs 15:2; Proverbs 20:1

- Talents – The queen of Sheba presented 120 talents of gold to king Solomon as a gift, (I Kings 10:10) and king Solomon received 666 talents of gold each year in tribute. (I Kings 10:14) A talent was a measurement of money in ancient times. What exactly was a talent? What different kinds of metal could a talent be? Were talents of great or little value? Did talents have a constant or fluctuating value? Using the value of gold today, try to calculate how much the queen's gift to the king would equal in our dollars and calculate the equivalent of Solomon's yearly tribute in our dollars.

 "Food For Thought": Puzzles

- Synonyms & Antonyms – Choose the words that are similar (synonyms) and that are opposite (antonyms) of wisdom and write them on the appropriate lines. There are six synonyms and six antonyms. If you need some help, you may use a dictionary or thesaurus. Answers are provided in the Answer Key.

good judgment	nonsense	foolishness	prudence
discernment	reason	stupidity	ignorance
inability	experience	bad judgment	understanding

Synonyms	Antonyms
_____	_____
_____	_____
_____	_____
_____	_____
_____	_____
_____	_____

- Crossword Puzzle – Answers are provided in the Answer Key.

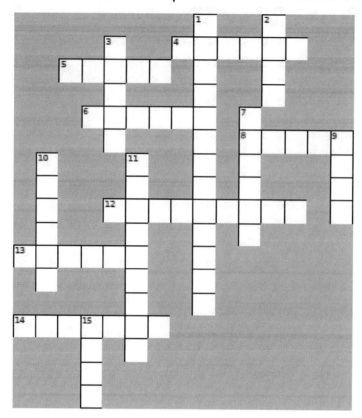

Across

4 Solomon was famous for his _____

5 The queen of Sheba spoke to Solomon about all that was in her _____

6 When the queen of Sheba saw all the wisdom of Solomon and all his prosperity, there was no more _____ in her

8 The kind of wood Solomon used for the steps of the temple

12 Capital city of Israel where Solomon reigned as king

13 The queen of Sheba said it was a true _____ which she heard of Solomon in her own country

14 What Solomon could not explain to the queen of Sheba

Down

1 The queen of Sheba said the Lord made Solomon king to do justice and _____

2 The queen of Sheba told Solomon, "Blessed be the _____ who delighted in you."

3 How the queen of Sheba described Solomon's servants

7 The queen of Sheba brought these animals bearing spices and gems

9 Hiram's fleet brought this from Ophir

10 The queen of Sheba brought these to King Solomon in great abundance

11 The queen of Sheba tested Solomon with these

15 The _____ was not told to the queen of Sheba regarding Solomon's wisdom and wealth

"Fruits Of Our Labor": Crafts

- Gem Frame - Proverbs 8:11 says that wisdom is better than rubies. This craft makes a pretty frame decorated with gems. You can do this two ways: Method #1 – For this craft you will need: A plain wooden frame, fake gemstones, paint color of your choice, and glue. Paint the frame with the color of your choice and let it dry. Next, glue fake gems all around the border and let them dry. Draw or paint Proverbs 8:11 to put inside the frame and display it. Method #2 - For this craft you will need: A plain wooden frame, clear glass craft rocks which are flat on one side, red glitter (or another color of your choice), and glue. First, pour your glitter into a small plate for easy "dipping". Next, use a sponge applicator to spread glue on the flat side of the rocks. Dip the rocks, glue side down, into the glitter, coating well. Let them dry completely. Finally, place a few drops of glue on the dried glitter side of the rocks and press firmly around the edge of the frame. Let dry. Draw or paint Proverbs 8:11 and place inside the frame.

  *You can use all red "gems" if you'd like since this verse says that wisdom is greater than rubies.

  *Instead of a painted frame, you can purchase a small chalkboard with a wooden frame and do the same craft, but simply write the verse in chalk on the board when finished.

- Cupcakes fit for royalty! - Let's get in the kitchen and have some fun! One of the items that the queen of Sheba brought to king Solomon as a gift was spices. She brought so many that it was said that there was never such an abundance of spices again in the kingdom of Israel. There are some wonderful spices that can be used for baking. Spices such as cinnamon, cloves, nutmeg, ginger, and cardamom, just to name a few. If you have these in your kitchen, get them out and smell each one in turn. Which one is your favorite? Now, prepare to make some delicious spice cupcakes. You can use either a boxed spice cake mix or a recipe from scratch. While they are baking and cooling, prepare frosting for them. Choose vanilla, cream cheese, maple, caramel, or another kind you like. The color purple often was worn by royalty because purple-dyed clothing was expensive and hard to come by. If using vanilla frosting, tint your frosting purple by using a purple frosting gel or by combining blue and red food coloring to make purple. When the cupcakes are completely cooled, frost them. To really make your cupcakes sparkle, sprinkle them with edible gold or silver glitter. (This can be found in the cake decorating departments at craft stores such as Michael's or Hobby Lobby.)

Lesson 7: The Shunammite Woman

A Woman of Hospitality

Text: II Kings 4:8-17

"Growing In The Word": Lesson Text & Discussion

Read II Kings 4:8. The prophet Elisha traveled frequently from town to town, doing the work of the Lord. He would often pass through the town of Shunem where a "notable" or "great" woman lived with her husband. This woman was either wealthy or a woman of position, and she was also thought to be a woman of great faith. She would always invite Elisha to stop at her house when he was in town so she could provide him with a good meal, and he would always accept her kind invitation. This Shunammite woman was showing Elisha hospitality. Do you know what the word "hospitality" means? (Allow for answers.) Hospitality is to receive guests, visitors, or strangers to our home in a friendly and generous way. Fixing a meal for Elisha was certainly a kind and hospitable thing for her to do, but she didn't stop there.

Read II Kings 4:9-10. How does the Shunammite woman describe Elisha to her husband? (She calls him a holy man of God.) It seems that Elisha wasn't just showing up at their house every once in a while but was making regular visits. Because of that, she had a wonderful idea. She presented her plan to her husband. What did she want to do for Elisha? (She wanted to build a room for him that he could stay in when he stopped by.) Think about when you travel with your family. Have you ever stopped at a hotel for the night? A hotel room usually contains the basic things a person needs to be comfortable for the night such as a bed, a table and chair, a bathroom, towels, a coffeemaker and maybe even a small refrigerator and microwave. What items did the Shunammite woman want to include in the room for Elisha? (A bed, a table, a chair and a lampstand) These items would be all that Elisha needed in order to be comfortable away from home. He would have a bed to sleep in, a table and chair to sit at in order to work or eat, and a lampstand to provide light at night.

Read II Kings 4:11-13. One day soon after this, Elisha came to the town of Shunem and went to visit his friends as usual. He was shown up to the special room made just for him, and he gratefully lay down on the bed and rested. He must have been so surprised and pleased when he saw all the effort that had been made for him to have his own comfortable room to stay in when he was in town. He was so thankful for the kindness, thoughtfulness, and generosity of the Shunammite woman that he was determined to give her something special in return. He told his servant to call the Shunammite woman to come before him. What was the name of Elisha's servant? (Gehazi) What was the first thing Elisha offered to do for the Shunammite woman? (He asked her if she wanted him to speak to the king or commander of the army on her behalf.) It seems that Elisha had some favor and influence with the king and could have used it to help the woman or her husband if she needed it. How did she answer him? (She said, "I dwell among my own people.") She is saying that she lives in peace among her neighbors and has no need for Elisha to speak to the king about anything for her. She is content. Elisha accepts this answer, but he is still determined to do something to thank her for her kindness and hospitality.

Read II Kings 4:14-17. This time, Elisha wonders aloud what can possibly be done for her, and his servant has a perfect answer. What did Gehazi say the Shunammite woman did not have? (He said she had no son.) This woman was childless, and her husband was old so it was likely she would never have any children. When Elisha heard this, he called her to him again and told her that by this time next year, she would have a little son to hold. What was her reaction? (She was so shocked, she couldn't believe it.) Did the prophet's words come true? (Yes!) A year later, she was blessed by God with a little boy of her own.

This all began when the Shunammite woman invited a stranger to her home to offer him a good meal. Later they became friends, and she could see what he needed and how she could provide it. It would help this prophet of God if he had a comfortable place to rest and work when he visited her town, so she went to great expense and effort to build and furnish a room just for him. Those are some of the important parts of showing hospitality to someone. It's easy (and fun) to invite friends over to our house for a snack or meal, and that is certainly showing hospitality as well, but it takes more effort to invite a stranger and then find out what needs they might have that you can provide for them in your home. It is also a special blessing to others when we show hospitality to someone who can't pay it back in any way. There is no shortage of who we can show hospitality to or how we can do it. We just need to open our eyes and look for opportunities.

The Shunammite woman is a great example of one who has a heart for hospitality. She teaches us what it means to open our homes, hands, and hearts to serve others.

Review Questions: (Answers are provided in the Answer Key.)

1. What does "hospitality" mean?

2. How is the Shunammite woman described?

3. How did the Shunammite woman show hospitality to Elisha at first?

4. How did she describe Elisha to her husband?

5. What four items did she include in the room for Elisha?

6. What did Elisha first offer to do for her in order to show her thanks for her hospitality?

7. Why did the Shunammite woman not accept Elisha's offer of him speaking to the king on her behalf?

8. Who was Gehazi, and what did he suggest?

9. What was the reaction of the Shunammite woman to the prophecy of Elisha?

10. Did the prophecy of Elisha concerning the Shunammite woman come true?

 "Putting Down Roots": Memory Work

- Memorize I Peter 4:9
- Memorize Hebrews 13:2

 "Farther Afield": Map Work

Map 4

- Locate the city of Shunem
- Locate Mt. Carmel

 "Harvest Fun": Games & Activities

- Brainstorm! - Brainstorm and make a list of people you would like to show hospitality to as well as what you would like to do for them. Would you like to invite a widow for tea, a single mom and her kids for a movie night, a missionary for a meal? Plan your work, then work your plan!

- Snacks & Goodies – If you've completed the brainstorming activity, now you have to think of some snacks and goodies you'd like to serve to your guests. Here are some recipes that are quick, easy, and delicious to get you started:

Pepperoni Dip

1 can of cream of mushroom soup

2 (8 oz.) bricks of cream cheese

8 oz. of pepperoni

In a small crockpot, place the bricks of cream cheese and pour the soup over them. Cut up the pepperoni into small pieces and scatter over the top of the soup. Let it cook on low for about an hour, then stir altogether to blend. Let it continue to cook on low for about 2 hours, stirring every 20 minutes or so. The oil from the pepperoni will eventually turn the dip a light orange color. Serve with crackers.

Fruit Salsa

2 kiwis, peeled and diced

2 Golden Delicious apples – peeled, cored and diced

1 pound strawberries, hulled and diced

2 T. sugar

1 T. brown sugar

3 T. fruit preserves, any flavor

In a large bowl, thoroughly mix all of the fruit, sugar, brown sugar, and fruit preserves. Cover and chill in the refrigerator for 30 minutes. Serve with cinnamon graham crackers.

Chocolate Chip Cookie Dough Dip

1 stick butter

1/3 cup brown sugar

1 tsp. vanilla extract

1 (8 oz.) pkg. cream cheese, softened

½ cup powdered sugar

¾ cup mini chocolate chips

In a saucepan, melt butter with brown sugar over medium heat. Stir continuously until the sugar is fully dissolved. Remove pan from heat and whisk in vanilla. Set aside to cool. In a bowl, beat the cream cheese and powdered sugar for 1 minute. Slowly beat in the cooled butter mixture and beat for one more minute. Stir in the chocolate chips. Place in a serving bowl and refrigerate. The dip will become pretty solid in the refrigerator so remove it 20-30 minutes before serving to soften. Serve with graham crackers, shortbread cookies, or Nilla wafers.

Triple Chocolate Brownies

1 small package instant chocolate pudding

1 pkg. chocolate cake mix

2 cups chocolate chips

In a large bowl, prepare pudding mix according to package directions. Pour in dry cake mix and blend well. Stir in the chocolate chips. Pour into a greased 9x13 pan. Bake at 350 degrees for 30-35 minutes or until the top springs lightly when touched.

"Digging Deeper": Research

- Elisha – Elisha is a fascinating prophet to study. We see one of the miracles he performed when he raised the Shunammite woman's son from the dead, but there is a great deal more we can learn about him. Research Elisha and try to answer the following questions about him: 1) What does his name mean? 2) What prophet was his mentor and whose position he filled? 3) From II Kings 2 – II Kings 6, see if you can find and list at least nine miracles Elisha performed. 4) What interesting incident happened in II Kings 2:23-24? 5) What miracle happened in II Kings 13:21 that involved Elisha after he was already dead?

- Genesis 18:1-8 – In this passage, we can read about another event where hospitality was demonstrated. Read the passage then answer the following questions: 1) Who showed hospitality? 2) To whom was it shown? 3) What were three ways hospitality was demonstrated?

 ## "Food For Thought": Puzzles

- Host & Hostesses – Choose the correct answer from the box and write it on the line. Answers are provided in the Answer Key.

Pharaoh – Genesis 45:16-20	Rahab – Joshua 2:1-16
Abraham – Genesis 18:1-8	Martha – Luke 10:38-42
Zaccheus – Luke 19:5-6	Lydia – Acts 16:14-15
Lot – Genesis 19:1-3	Island Natives – Acts 28:2
Publius – Acts 28:7	Philippian Jailer – Acts 16:25-34

1. Who served a meal to three men only realizing later that two were angels and the third was the Lord? _____

2. Who showed kindness by kindling a fire for some cold, recently shipwrecked people?

_____

3. Who received Jesus joyfully at his house when Jesus announced his intention to visit him? _____

4. Who offered the best of the land to Jacob and his family? _____

_____

5. Who let two foreign men lodge at her house and gave them protection from the king?

_____

6. Who insisted upon two angels spending the night at his house and prepared a feast for them? _____

7. Who begged Paul and his companions to stay at her house after her baptism?

_____

8. What important citizen of Malta courteously entertained Paul and others for three days? _____

9. Who welcomed Jesus into her home but was distracted with all of the serving?

_____

10. After Paul and Silas' miraculous release from prison, who washed their stripes and served them a meal at his house? _____

- Sequence – In order to do this puzzle, you must first read about the events that happened to the son of the Shunammite woman in II Kings 4:18-37. Then read the following statements, and place them in the correct order by numbering them from 1-10. Answers are provided in the Answer Key.

_____ 1. The woman went up and laid her son on the bed of the prophet.

_____ 2. The woman and her husband made a room for Elisha's use.

_____ 3. The little boy cried "My head, my head!"

_____ 4. Gehazi laid the prophet's staff on the child's face.

_____ 5. The woman fell at the feet of Elisha and picked up her son.

_____ 6. Elisha asked the woman, "What can I do for you?"

_____ 7. The man asked his wife why she was going to see the prophet.

_____ 8. The child sneezed seven times and opened his eyes.

_____ 9. Gehazi tried to push the woman away, but Elisha stopped him.

_____ 10. Gehazi told Elisha that the woman had no son.

"Fruits Of Our Labor": Crafts

• Friendship Quilt – When the Shunammite woman furnished the room for her friend Elisha, perhaps she made a homemade blanket for his bed as well. It's nice to have homemade touches when showing hospitality to someone. This is a fun project that you could make for a guest room in your own home or as a gift to give to someone. For this quilt you will need: 8 large solid color t-shirts (use old ones or find cheap ones at a thrift store), fabric paint, sewing scissors, a ruler, and a cutting board. First, you need to measure and cut out 16 t-shirt squares measuring 12 inches square. This would be 2 squares from each t-shirt, possibly 4 if you use X-Large size shirts. Chalk is helpful to mark your measurements and show you where to cut. Next, take each square and cut a 2 inch fringe all the way around, one inch apart, leaving a 2 inch block at each corner. Make a diagonal cut in each of these corner blocks. You will be using this fringe to tie your squares together later. After all of your squares are cut and fringed, decide how you would like to decorate the squares with your fabric paint. You may want to invite different family members or friends to press their hand in the fabric paint and place their hand print on a square. You can paint their name underneath their hand print if you'd like. You could also place your hand print next to theirs on the square. (This would especially be fun if some of the people who helped decorate the quilt get to be guests in your home later on and sleep under the quilt!) After your squares are decorated or painted, let everything dry completely and then you can start assembling your quilt. Choose four squares and start tying them together in a row. Set them aside and tie four more squares together in a row. Then you can tie the two rows together, but don't tie the corner pieces yet! Make double knots with each tie to keep it from coming undone. If you need to make your fringe a little longer, just snip another 1/4 inch with the scissors. The squares will really start to shrink up as you tie. You can gently stretch them and pull them back into a square shape. Finish tying your other two rows of four squares each, one row at a time, then add each row to the quilt, leaving the corner pieces of each square untied. Once all of the rows are tied together into one big quilt, you can begin tying the corner pieces. To tie the corner pieces, take one each of the triangular corner pieces that are diagonally opposite each other and tie. Leave their partners free. Take one each of the other corner pieces that are diagonally opposite each other and tie them. You should end up with two knots and four corner fringes free at each of the seams where four squares meet. Now you're done!

- Design a room – The Shunammite woman put great thought and care into the room she and her husband provided for Elisha. They considered what he might need to be comfortable and to work. Imagine you are going to build and design a room for guests such as traveling missionaries, families who need temporary shelter from natural disasters (such as hurricanes, fires, etc.), homeless people who need temporary shelter, or any others you can think of. Now depending on who your guests might be, think about what things they would need to be comfortable and/or to work. For example, some guests would need a place to plug in and charge devices so they can communicate with others far away or be able to work on their laptop. Just like Elisha had a table to sit and work in his room, your "working" guests might appreciate a small desk or table for a work space. If your guests include children, those families would probably appreciate a basket or shelves of toys and books for children in their guest room. Draw your room plan design making sure to include all furniture and items you have in your plan. To be able to "move" things around on your design, use a legal size pad of graph paper to draw the room. Draw pieces of furniture on a separate sheet of plain paper in shapes such as a large rectangle for a bed, a square for a night stand, etc., and cut the shapes out. Arrange them on the graph paper where you think you want them, and if you're not happy with the layout, move the pieces around until you like the design. The point of hospitality is to be mindful of the needs of others as you serve them.

Lesson 8: Athaliah

A Woman of Wickedness

Text: II Chronicles 21:4-6; 22:2-4, 10-12; 23:1-21

"Growing In The Word": Lesson Text & Discussion

Read II Chronicles 21:4-6. Jehoshaphat was one of the kings who had reigned over the southern kingdom of Judah. He was a good king who had tried to follow the Lord faithfully. His son, Jehoram, became the next king after his father's death. Would you say he was like his father? Why or why not? (No! He killed all of his brothers and other princes of Israel.) Why would he do such a thing? This was a way that kings would try to secure their thrones. They removed all threats of someone usurping (taking over) usually by killing them. In this case, Jehoram kills all of his own brothers so there's no chance any of them would try to take his place. How old was he when he began to reign and how many years did he rule? (He was 32 years old when he became king, and he reigned 8 years.) We see one of the reasons he rejected following in his father's footsteps in this passage. To whom was he married? (The daughter of Ahab and Jezebel) Her name was Athaliah, and she was a princess from the northern kingdom of Israel. Her parents were evil people, and she was exactly like them. She married a prince of Judah, and then became queen of that nation. Instead of following the good example of his own father, Jehoram followed the example of his wife's father and chose to do much evil in the sight of God.

Read II Chronicles 22:2-4. After the short reign of Jehoram, Ahaziah reigned in his place. He was the son of Jehoram and Athaliah. His reign was even shorter than his father's. How long did he rule as king? (One year) He was a chip off the old block by following in the footsteps of one of his grandfathers. Did he reign as a good king like his grandfather Jehoshaphat, or did he follow the example of his wicked grandfather Ahab? (He was like his grandfather Ahab – an evil king.) Ahab was the son of Omri who was another evil king of Israel. Athaliah was the granddaughter of Omri and the daughter of Ahab. Ahaziah had a bad example from his father, grandfather, etc., but who does this passage say actually counseled him to do wickedly? (His mother, Athaliah) As a wife, she influenced her husband, Jehoram to commit evil, and as a mother, she was giving advice to her son on how to do wickedly. She was definitely not a nice woman, and we'll see as we keep reading just how evil she really was.

Read II Chronicles 22:10-12. After reigning as king for one short year, Ahaziah has died. What is the first thing Athaliah, the queen mother, does? (She destroys all the royal heirs.)

Remember how her husband, Jehoram, did something similar by killing all of his brothers? Now Athaliah sees her chance to rule unopposed as queen. Was she successful in wiping out all of the royal heirs? (No) She missed one. Joash was an infant son of Ahaziah. While Athaliah was rounding up and destroying the royal heirs, someone was wise enough and brave enough to hide this little prince from her. Who hid him? (Jehoshabeath) Jehoshabeath was a daughter of King Jehoram and sister to Ahaziah. She was married to a priest named Jehoiada. Jehoshabeath hid little Joash and his nurse in a bedroom in the temple quarters. How long was Joash kept hidden? (Six years) Who reigned over Judah during this time? (Athaliah) Athaliah believed all the royal heirs to be dead so she saw a clear path to the throne for herself.

Read II Chronicles 23:1-3. Six years have passed and little Joash is now seven years old. It is time for the rightful king to take his place on the throne. Jehoiada the priest is going to take charge of organizing all of this. Do you remember who he was married to? (Jehoshabeath, the one who hid Joash) In this chapter, several covenants will be made. What is a covenant? (Allow answers.) A covenant is an agreement between two people or groups of people. One of the covenants that was made was between the people of Judah and Joash. Some of the leaders of the people gathered in the temple where little Joash was and promised to set him on the throne as the rightful king who they would follow and serve. They refer to Joash as one of the sons of David, but Ahaziah was his father. What are they talking about? When David was king of Israel over one hundred years earlier, God had promised him that he would always have an heir on the throne. Joash was a direct descendant of David, and the only living male heir at this time. The people of Judah knew that because of the promise of God to King David, Joash was the rightful king.

Read II Chronicles 23:4-7. Jehoiada the priest begins to lay out his plan to protect the king during this coronation. Remember, Athaliah is reigning as queen, and she thought she had killed all of the royal heirs. She will **not** be happy at what is about to take place so young Joash must be securely protected. Jehoiada commands all of the priests and Levites to take up stations at strategic areas, then he commands a portion of the Levites to completely surround the king. What were they to be holding in their hands? (Weapons) [Side note: All priests had to come from the tribe of Levi and were Levites, but not all Levites were priests. Some of them served in other ways at the temple as well, they just didn't hold the office of priest.] What order did Jehoiada give to the Levites who were personally guarding Joash? (He ordered them to kill anyone who tried to enter the temple who was unauthorized and might harm the king. These armed guards were never to leave the king's side.

Read II Chronicles 23:8-11. Not only were the Levites armed who were to personally guard Joash, but Jehoiada also armed captains of hundreds with spears and shields. Which king had these weapons originally belonged to? (King David) All the guards are in place. Now it is time for Joash to be brought out of hiding and crowned king in God's house, the temple. After the crown is placed on Joash's head, what was he given? (The Testimony) He was given a copy of the law of Moses as each king of Israel was to have his own personal copy of the law. (See Deuteronomy 17:18-20) If Joash is to be a successful king who will be faithful to God, he will need the scriptures to guide him. Next, Jehoiada and his sons anointed Joash. They would have anointed him with oil showing that this young man was God's choice to be the leader of His people. What did they shout as they anointed Joash king? ("Long live the king!")

Read II Chronicles 23:12-13. What day of the week is it when these things take place? (It is the Sabbath day, which is on Saturday.) This is the day of worship for the Jews which means that the people would be gathering at the temple to worship the Lord. Athaliah may not have been alarmed at the number of people flocking to the temple, but she is greatly alarmed when she hears what's going on. She heard the people shouting and praising the king. Probably not believing her ears, she runs to the temple to see what's taking place, and there he is – Joash, crowned king, standing by the temple entrance. What were the people at the temple doing? (They were singing, praising the king, blowing trumpets.) Such a clamor was in the air! Shouting, singing, instruments playing...everyone is so happy and excited to see the new king, the rightful king. What did Athaliah do? (She tore her clothes and shouted "Treason!") She is just beside herself! This was never supposed to happen! She thought she had secured her position as queen, but now she discovers that the people had been hiding and protecting a royal heir from her all this time. She is furious! But before she can do anything, Jehoiada already has in mind what the armed men will do to her.

Read II Chronicles 23:14-15. The armed guards were ordered by Jehoiada to take Athaliah out of the temple and kill her. No blood was to be shed in the house of God, but Athaliah, the real traitor, is going to be executed for the blood which she has shed. Where is she killed? (She is killed at the king's house.) Was anyone else ordered to be killed? (Anyone who showed loyalty to Athaliah by trying to follow her was to be killed as well.)

Read II Chronicles 23:16-21. Now we read about another covenant being made. This one is between the people (including the king) and the Lord. The people are all in agreement that they will be God's people. This means they have a heart to follow the Lord faithfully and do His will. Athaliah was an idol worshiper like her parents and grandfather before her. They all worshiped the false god Baal, and while Athaliah was queen she did all that she could to promote the worship of Baal and destroy the worship of the one true God. Now that she is dead and gone, the priests commit to promoting worship of God, Jehoiada promises that the king will be raised to be faithful to God, and the people all agree to these things. To follow through on their new commitment, they start by tearing down the temple of Baal. Who was executed? (Mattan, the priest of Baal) The people are determined to rid their land of idol worship and all of the bad influences of Athaliah. The next step Jehoiada takes is to place all the proper people in charge of the temple services, sacrifices, and worship just as the Lord had commanded it in the law of Moses. Finally, Joash is brought to the house of the king and placed on the throne. What was the reaction of all the people of the land? (They rejoiced.) They are so happy to be rid of Athaliah! Nobody is grieving at her death; no one is sorry that she is gone. Their nation is finally rid of a woman who rejected God and practiced evil continually. She has been replaced with the true king who will follow the Lord faithfully and lead the people to do the same.

II Chronicles 24:7 describes Athaliah as *"that wicked woman."* She had an opportunity to help her husband be a good king, to be a good mother to her son and counsel him how to rule wisely. She could have been a sweet grandmother and faithful servant in the Lord's kingdom, but instead she chose time after time after time to do wickedly. How sad.

<u>Review Questions</u>: (Answers are provided in the Answer Key.)

1. Who was Athaliah's husband?

2. Who were Athaliah's parents?

3. Who was Athaliah's son?

4. Which kingdom did her husband and son reign over?

5. What kind of king was Ahaziah (good or evil), and who gave him advice on how to reign?

6. How long did Ahaziah reign as king?

7. What was the first thing Athaliah did after her son had died?

8. Who was Joash, and what did Jehoshabeath do to him?

9. Who was Jehoshabeath's father?   Brother?   Husband?

10. How long was Joash hidden, and where was he hidden?

11. Who ruled over the nation of Judah during this time?

12. Which king was Joash a direct descendant of?

13. What had God promised this king over one hundred years earlier?

14. Who did Jehoiada place around the king to guard him?

15. What did they have in their hands?

16. On what day of the week was Joash crowned king?

17. After the crown was placed on his head, what was given to Joash?

18. What did the people cry out when Joash was anointed king?

19. What did Athaliah cry out when she discovered what was going on?

20. What happened to Athaliah the day Joash was crowned king?

21. What was the covenant the people made after Athaliah had died?

22. What false god did Athaliah worship?

23. What did the people tear down in the city?

24. Who was executed there?

25. What was the reaction of the people to Joash taking his place on the throne and Athaliah's death?

 "Putting Down Roots": Memory Work

- Memorize Proverbs 16:18

- Memorize the kings (and queen, if you count Athaliah) of the southern kingdom of Judah: Rehoboam, Abijah, Asa, Jehoshaphat, Jehoram, Ahaziah, Athaliah, Joash, Amaziah, Azariah (Uzziah), Jotham, Ahaz, Hezekiah, Manasseh, Amon, Josiah, Jehoahaz, Jehoiakim, Jehoiachin, Zedekiah

"Farther Afield": Map Work
Map 4

- Locate the region of Judah

- Locate the city of Jerusalem

- Draw a small symbol of the temple next to the city of Jerusalem

"Harvest Fun": Games & Activities

- Newspaper activity – Pretend you are a newspaper reporter living in the time of the divided kingdom of Israel. Athaliah would have been front page news! Write a newspaper story of these events including the answers to the questions who, what, when, where, and why in your story. Be sure to fact check with the scriptures. You can be creative as you'd like with this, designing an actual newspaper that could include advertisements, local events, and/or interviews with other interesting Bible characters from this lesson.

- Act it Out! - The crowning of King Joash and death of Athaliah is a great Bible event to act out. Go all out with props and costumes, gathering as many family and friends as you can to create this scene. Remember the crowd shouts, "Long live the king!" and cheers as the crown is placed on the head of Joash, and upon hearing this Athaliah dramatically tears her clothes and cries out, "Treason! Treason!"

"Digging Deeper": Research

- Ahab's Family Tree – Athaliah was the daughter of Ahab, a king of Israel, but she reigned in Judah. So…how did that happen? Research the family line of Ahab. If it helps, draw out a family tree on paper and fill in the names. Who was Ahab's father and in which kingdom did he reign? Who did Ahab marry? Who was their daughter? Whom did she marry and in which kingdom did he reign? Which of their sons reigned? Which of their grandsons reigned in Judah?

- The Divided Kingdom – The first three kings of Israel were Saul, David and Solomon, and they ruled over what was known as the united kingdom of Israel. After the death of Solomon, the kingdom split in two. Ten tribes of Israel made up the northern kingdom and two tribes made up the southern kingdom. All the names of the kings and who ruled where can be a little (or a lot!) confusing. Make a chart for the divided kingdom. This will be a great study resource for you to hang on to as well. Make the front of the sheet a chart for the northern kingdom of Israel and the back of the sheet for the southern kingdom of Judah. At the top of each page, list the following headings: Name of Ruler, Length of Reign, Good or Bad? Now, number down each page to list the names of the kings. Draw a down arrow from one name to the one below it if it is a father/son. Under the "Good or Bad?" heading, this will be determined by God's evaluation of the ruler found in scripture. For instance, it may say, "*He did evil in the sight of the Lord*", or "*He walked in the ways of* _____ (another evil ruler)." Or it will say something like, "*He did what was right in the sight of the Lord.*" When you finish this project, look at each chart. What are some interesting things you notice? (Hint: dynasties, number of good vs. bad rulers, etc.)

"Food For Thought": Puzzles

- Before or After? - Athaliah seized the throne of the kingdom of Judah and reigned as queen for six years. Read carefully each of the following statements and decide if they happened before or after she seized the throne. Answers are provided in the Answer Key.

1. Mattan, the priest of Baal, was killed. _____

2. Athaliah cried out, "Treason! Treason!" _____

Growing Up in God's Word: Women of the Bible

3. Ahaziah was counseled by his mother to do wickedly. _____

4. Jehoshabeath hid Joash. _____

5. Athaliah married Jehoram, king of Judah. _____

6. Jehoram killed all of his brothers. _____

7. Joash was crowned king. _____

8. Jehoiada the priest appointed guards for Joash. _____

9. Athaliah killed all of the royal heirs to the throne. _____

10. Ahaziah died. _____

- Who Am I? - Read each of the following clues, choose the correct answer from the box, then write it on the line. Answers are provided in the Answer Key.

Jehoiada	Joash	Athaliah	David
Ahaziah	Omri	Jehoshabeath	Ahab
	Jehoram	Mattan	

1. I am the wife of a priest. I hid Joash when he was a baby. _____

2. I am the son of Jehoram. I reigned as king of Judah for 1 year. _____

3. My granddaughter is Athaliah. I was a king of Israel. _____

4. I am the wife of Jehoram and mother of Ahaziah. _____

5. I am the priest who ordered the death of Athaliah. _____

6. I am a grandson of king Jehoram who became king when I was 7 years old.

_____

7. I reigned as a king of Judah. My son was Ahaziah. _____

© 2018, Pryor Convictions Media, Paul & Heather Pryor, St. Petersburg, FL

8. I reigned as a king of Israel. My daughter was Athaliah. _____

9. I am a king of Israel and Judah, and Joash was one of my descendants. My weapons were handed out to the soldiers who were guarding Joash. _____

10. I am a priest of Baal. I was killed after Athaliah was put to death. _____

"Fruits Of Our Labor": Crafts

- Design a crown – Athaliah seized the throne and made herself queen of the kingdom of Judah. Do you think she wore a crown? We know that little king Joash did because the crowd shouted "Long live the king!" as a crown was placed upon his head. There have been many types of crowns throughout history, some very simple using items from nature and others very elaborate and expensive. If you could wear a crown, what would you want it to look like? Try your hand at designing a crown. Think about the shape you would like, any favorite colors and any items you would like to incorporate. Do you like the thought of a leafy vine woven around your head? Or do you like the thought of glittering jewels? Be creative and original with your design! For even more fun, do this activity with some friends and compare crowns when everyone is finished. Do any two look exactly alike?

- Hide Joash! - Athaliah was one not-so-nice grandmother! Joash was carefully hidden from her as a baby and young child in the house of God which was the temple. For this craft, you are going to hide baby Joash in a baking soda block temple, then free him when it is time for his coronation! You will need baking soda, vinegar, and a small plastic baby doll (these can be found at craft stores in the cake decorating section). First, you will need to pour baking soda into a bowl and start adding water to it slowly, stirring to make a very thick paste. You can test the thickness by scooping up a section and squeezing it in your hand. If it sticks together and holds its shape, it's perfect! Add more water or baking soda as needed to get the correct consistency. Now, take half of the mixture and mold a square or rectangle shape. Place the baby doll in the middle and press down gently. Mold the remaining half of the mixture over the bottom half until you've covered the baby and have one solid block. Place the block on an ungreased baking sheet, and bake at 200 degrees for 3 hours. Let it cool completely. If you'd like your block to look more like a temple, you can paint it and let it dry. Before the next step, you might want to take a picture of your "temple" because it's about to disappear! Pour vinegar in a large bowl. Carefully place your temple into the vinegar and watch what starts to happen. Use tongs or a spoon to help break up chunks. Once you see little Joash, use some tongs to fish him out. He needs to get cleaned up so he can be crowned king!

Lesson 9: The Proverbs 31 Woman
A Woman of Virtue

Text: Proverbs 31:10-31

"Growing In The Word": Lesson Text & Discussion

Read Proverbs 31:10. If you look back at verse one of this chapter, you will see that these are the words of King Lemuel that were taught to him by his mother. His mother knew the importance of her son finding a good wife so she taught him what kind of woman that wife should be. What kind of a wife is worth much more than valuable rubies? (A virtuous wife) What does virtuous mean? To be virtuous means to be good and pure, to live righteously. Do you think virtue is an important quality for a wife (or any woman) to have?

Read Proverbs 31:11-12. What will a virtuous wife always do for her husband for as long as she lives? (Good) A wife should never do evil toward her husband or treat him badly in any way. She should always treat him well and do right towards him. When a man has a wife such as this, he can trust her. He will never have to worry about what she is doing or what evil or bad thing she may be plotting behind his back. For example, when he earns his paycheck and puts it in the bank to take care of his family, he can trust his wife to use the money wisely instead of using it foolishly or even doing something evil with it like stealing it.

Read Proverbs 31:13. Back in Bible times, having clothes to wear was not as simple as going to the store to buy them. Everything was made by hand and the cloth to make the clothes had to be handmade as well. Wool was sheared from sheep and then carded, spun and woven into cloth which could then be cut into garments to wear. Flax is a plant which was used to make linen. Working with wool and flax would be time-consuming, but did the virtuous woman seem to mind? (No) How did she do her work? (Willingly) She did not go about grumbling and complaining but was cheerful as she did her household tasks.

Read Proverbs 31:14-15. These two verses deal with how the virtuous woman provided the food for everyone in the house. A wise woman will be thrifty and frugal, that is she doesn't waste money but tries to find good deals. This woman may have had to travel to several different markets in her city to find the best deals on food. She also made sure that the food she provided for her family was good quality food. Some of her food purchases may have been brought in by merchant ships which would mean she could buy good food that may not have been available in the area where she lived. What time did she get up each day? (While it was still night) She was up before the sun, starting the day with cooking. She wasn't one to sleep in late each day while the members of the household fended for themselves and got their own breakfast. She took the responsibility of seeing that every member of her household, including servants, was fed and fed well.

Read Proverbs 31:16-19. We have already seen that this virtuous woman works hard and willingly. Apparently, she also makes things that she can sell. She does quality work that she is not ashamed of and makes a good profit from her sales. What does she buy? (A field) What does she plant? (A vineyard) This shows us more of her wisdom and industry. She spends her money wisely on something that can be put to good use for her family. She plants grape vines which would provide fruit for her family's use or even to sell in the marketplace. What does not go out at night? (Her lamp) She is willing to work long hours to finish everything that needs to be done.

Read Proverbs 31:20. What quality do we see in the virtuous woman from this verse? (Compassion) Compassion is feeling pity and concern for others and then acting on it by helping them in some way. This woman is not only mindful of taking good care of her family, but she cares about other people as well and tries to help them in any way that she can. Who in particular does she help? (The poor) She shares the resources that God has blessed her with whether it be food, clothing, money, etc.

Read Proverbs 31:21-22. The virtuous woman is a woman who prepares. She thinks ahead to what her family will need and then provides it ahead of time. When winter comes, she doesn't worry about her children shivering in thin clothing because she has already prepared warm clothing of scarlet for them. Scarlet is a deep red color which might make you think, "How can red clothes keep you warm?" Good question! This word, *scarlet*, refers to a double thickness of cloth or in other words, warm clothes! The virtuous woman also makes tapestry which would be used in different ways to decorate a home. They could be made into wall hangings or pillows. She obviously has good taste and likes to make her home look beautiful, comfortable, and inviting. What is her clothing made of? (Fine linen and purple) Both of these would be expensive cloth of good quality. Her clothing is not cheap and poorly made but tasteful and of good quality.

Read Proverbs 31:23. Now we learn a little bit about her husband. Where does he sit? (Among the elders of the land) Her husband is some type of elder or ruler in the land. He is a person of high standing in the community and one who is honored and looked up to. Because the virtuous woman handles things so well at home and her husband has full trust in her, he is able to go about his business each day and do his own work.

Read Proverbs 31:24. What does she do with the linen garments that she makes? (She sells them.) We have already seen how the virtuous woman works willingly with her hands to spin and weave materials like wool and flax. Now we see that she also makes linen garments and sashes which she sells. These would be high quality clothing items that would be expensive and bring a good price. It is obvious from the type of clothing her family wore and the decorations in her home that her family was not poor, so why do you think she makes items to sell? (Answers will vary.)

Read Proverbs 31:25. Strength and honor may sound like funny clothes to wear, but both of these are referring to the kind of woman that she is. Strength is not referring to how strong she is physically but to her strength of character. She is called a virtuous woman – she is a woman who is righteous, clean, wholesome, and pure. Because of that, she is looked up to and honored by others. She has a good name or reputation among people, and they respect her. How does she view the future? (She rejoices or laughs at it.) This woman does not walk around wringing her hands and worrying about everything that might happen tomorrow or next month or next year. She can laugh at the future because she feels secure. She trusts in God to provide and does her part by working hard and preparing things such as food, clothing and money. She has no need to worry about the future. She can relax and enjoy the life she is blessed with.

Read Proverbs 31:26. This verse describes the way the virtuous woman talks. Would you say that she is a gossip, complainer, or shallow person? (No) She speaks gently and kindly. She thinks before she speaks and chooses her words carefully so she doesn't say something foolish. She is wise with her words and careful to be kind. Do you think she had to work hard to talk like this? (Answers will vary.) Speaking with wisdom and kindness takes practice each and every day, but if we work hard at it, it can become a good habit and a way of life for us just like it was for the virtuous woman.

Read Proverbs 31:27. The virtuous woman is not selfish. She thinks of the needs of others before herself and puts them first. Her family and others in her household are important to her. She works hard to supply everything that they need whether it be good food each day or warm clothing or a clean, comfortable home to live in. She is always watching and alert to anything her family needs. What does the virtuous woman never eat? (The bread of idleness) What is idleness? Idleness is laziness. It is sitting around not working or being productive at anything. This woman is not idle! She is always busy at good and important things such as taking good care of her family and helping the poor. She can be a good example to remember whenever we feel tempted to be idle and lazy.

Read Proverbs 31:28-29. How do the virtuous woman's husband and children feel about her? (Her children call her blessed, and her husband praises her.) Those who love her and know her best give her respect and praise. She is treated this way because she makes home happy not just by what she does but by what she is. They all see and appreciate her true value. Remember in the beginning of this lesson we learned that the worth of a virtuous woman is far above rubies? Her husband especially realizes this as he sings her praises. He basically says that there are a lot of wonderful women in the world, but his wife outdoes them all! High praise indeed!

Read Proverbs 31:30-31. Many women in the world today are praised because of their great beauty, their outward looks. It doesn't seem to matter what they are like on the inside. But verse 30 tells us that outward beauty can be vain (unimportant or shallow) if that woman has no inner beauty. The virtuous woman that we have been studying about was beautiful from the inside out because she feared (respected and reverenced) the Lord. She will be praised because she is a faithful follower of God. What will praise her in the gates? (Her own works) In John 15:8 Jesus talked about "bearing good fruit" and how we can know people by the kind of fruit they bear (Matthew 7:17-20). He was talking about actions. We are known by what we do. People can determine if we are a good person or an evil person. In the same way, the virtuous woman was known by her "fruit." Her good works and actions were seen by others each day and it showed everyone the kind of person she was.

This woman of the Bible serves as a good example to all of us as to what it means to be a virtuous woman. She worked hard, she was kind and gentle, she was compassionate and helpful, but most of all, she loved God and followed Him.

Review Questions: (Answers are provided in the Answer Key.)

1. Whose mother taught him the importance of a virtuous wife?

2. What is a virtuous wife worth to her husband?

3. What will a virtuous wife do for her husband all the days of his life?

4. In what way did the virtuous woman work with her hands?

5. What time did the virtuous woman get up each day?

6. What did the virtuous woman buy with her profits, and what did she plant?

7. How did the virtuous woman treat the poor and needy?

8. What does the word *scarlet* refer to?

9. What did the virtuous woman decorate her home with?

10. What was her clothing made out of?

11. Where did her husband sit each day?

12. What did the virtuous woman sell?

13. How did the virtuous woman view the future?

14. What did she open her mouth with?

15. How did she speak to others?

16. What did the virtuous woman never eat?

17. What did the virtuous woman's children call her?

18. How did the virtuous woman's husband feel about her?

19. What does Proverbs 31:30 say is vain or useless?

20. What kind of woman will be praised?

 "Putting Down Roots": Memory Work

- Memorize Proverbs 31:10

- Memorize Proverbs 31:30

 "Add a Leaf": Words to know – There are no mapping exercises for this lesson so instead, look up and write the definitions of the following words from the lesson.

- Virtuous

- Flax

- Spindle

- Distaff

- Tapestry

- Idleness

"Harvest Fun": Games & Activities

- Scavenger Hunt – This game is for one or more players or two teams. Each individual or team will be given a list of items. Set a time limit of your choosing (3 – 5 minutes), and see who can find all of the items (or the most) on the list before time is up. All of the list items are referred to in some way in this lesson. <u>List items</u>: candle, red clothing, piece of bread, fruit, thread, yarn, packet of seeds, winter coat, belt, money, purple clothing, jewelry, pair of eyeglasses. After the game is over, either award bonus points if a player or team can tell how each item relates to the virtuous woman, or simply discuss these for a review. Candle – her candle (or lamp) does not go out at night, red clothing – her household is clothed with scarlet, piece of bread – she does not eat the bread of idleness, fruit – give her the fruit of her hands, thread – she looks for flax and flax fibers are used to make linen, yarn – she looks for wool which is spun into yarn, packet of seeds – she plants a vineyard, winter coat – she isn't afraid of snow, belt – she makes sashes for the merchants, money – she buys a field, purple clothing – her clothing is fine linen and purple, jewelry – she is worth more than rubies, pair of eyeglasses – she watches over the ways of her household.

- Honor a virtuous woman – Think about the women you know who are close to you such as your mom, grandmother, aunt, friend at church, etc. Is there a particular one that stands out to you as being a good example of a godly woman like the virtuous woman of Proverbs 31? Think of a way to show her honor. For example, you could invite her over for tea and have some homemade cookies to serve her. Or you could give her a gift of a pretty tea cup and saucer. Place a tea bag inside the tea cup along with a print-out of Proverbs 31:30 rolled up and tied with a pretty ribbon.

"Digging Deeper": Research

- Spinning Wool – Do some research as to how wool is spun into yarn using a spinning wheel and how it is done with modern machines. Write down the steps in each process.

- Making Tapestry – A tapestry is a heavy cloth woven with beautiful colors to show a scene or design. It was usually hung on a wall for decoration. How were tapestries made? Were they easy or difficult to make? Do you think they would be quick to make or would take a long time? See if you can find a picture of "The Bayeux Tapestry". It is a famous (huge!) tapestry that shows the Norman conquest of England and the Battle of Hastings which took place in the year 1066.

"Food For Thought": Puzzles

- True or False – Read the following statements about the virtuous woman and decide if they are true or false. Answers are provided in the Answer Key.

_____ 1. She is worth more than rubies.

_____ 2. She plants a cornfield.

_____ 3. She is afraid of snow.

_____ 4. She is compassionate to the needy.

_____ 5. Her children are afraid of her.

_____ 6. She does her husband good.

_____ 7. Her clothing is fine linen and blue.

_____ 8. She speaks wisely and with kindness.

_____ 9. She gets her food close by at the market.

_____10. The merchants praise her.

- Complete the proverb – Match the beginning of the proverb in the left column with its ending in the right column. Answers are provided in the Answer Key.

_____ 1. She perceives that her merchandise is good,

_____ 2. Her children rise up and call her blessed

_____ 3. She does him good and not evil

_____ 4. She watches over the ways of her household

_____ 5. Many daughters have done well,

_____ 6. She seeks wool and flax

_____ 7. Strength and honor are her clothing

_____ 8, She is like the merchant ships,

_____ 9. She makes tapestry for herself;

_____10. Charm is deceitful and beauty is vain,

a) and works willingly with her hands.

b) but a woman who fears the Lord, she shall be praised.

c) she brings her food from afar.

d) she shall rejoice in time to come.

e) her clothing is fine linen and purple.

f) and her lamp does not go out at night.

g) and does not eat the bread of idleness.

h) all the days of her life.

i) but you excel them all.

j) her husband also, and he praises her.

"Fruits Of Our Labor": Crafts

- Tea Mix – Here are two easy recipes to make a delicious tea mix that can be put in jars which you decorate.

<u>Friendship Tea Mix</u>

18 oz. orange breakfast drink mix   1/2 cup powdered lemonade mix

1 cup instant iced tea mix	2 1/2 tsp. cinnamon
1 cup sugar	1 tsp. ground cloves

In a large bowl, combine all ingredients until well-blended. Store in an airtight container for up to six months. To make a cup of hot tea: Use 4 1/2 tsp. of mix to one 6-8 oz. cup of boiling water.   Yield: About 5 cups of mix

<u>Chai Tea Mix</u>

1 cup dry milk powder	2 tsp. ginger
1 cup powdered non-dairy creamer	2 tsp. ground cinnamon
1 cup French vanilla creamer (dry)	1 tsp. ground cloves
2 1/2 cups sugar	1 tsp. ground cardamom
1 1/2 cups unsweetened tea mix	

In a large bowl, combine all ingredients until well-blended. Store in an airtight container. To make a cup of hot tea: Use 2 heaping teaspoons in one 6-8 oz. cup of boiling water. This link provides instructions for a gift basket for your tea mixes. http://pryorconvictions.com/chai-tea-mixtea-for-two-gift-basket/ This would make a nice gift to give a woman you would like to honor from the "Games/Activities" assignment. To give these mixes as gifts, either follow the directions in the link provided, or simply place tea mix in a clean, dry Mason jar then tie a pretty ribbon around the top and attach a label with the name of the tea and instructions on how to make a cup of tea using the mix. (Label templates can be found in Appendix B.)

- Illustrate Proverbs 31:22 in whatever way you'd like: Painting, drawing, chalk, etc.

Lesson 10: Three "Negative Nellies" - Lot's Wife, Mrs. Job & Maacah

Women of Discouragement & Disobedience

Text: Genesis 19:1-3, 15-26; Job 1:1-3, 8-22; 2:1-10; I Kings 15:1-3, 9-13

"Growing In The Word": Lesson Text & Discussion

Before we get into this lesson, you might be wondering just what exactly is a "negative Nellie"? Well, negative is the opposite of positive. To be positive is to be one who thinks well about things and about other people. A positive person is one who encourages, does not complain, and tries to do good. A negative person is the opposite. She thinks bad about others, she complains, she discourages, and she can be disobedient. A "negative Nellie" became a common slang term that was used to describe someone with these bad qualities. In this lesson, we will look at three women who could, unfortunately, be described in this way.

Read Genesis 19:1-3. Lot was the nephew of Abraham, and he and his family lived in the city of Sodom. Who arrived in the city at evening? (Two angels) These angels looked like men who were just traveling; Lot didn't realize they were angels. When Lot saw them, what did he offer to them? (He offered hospitality.) Lot was offering these strangers a place to sleep and refresh themselves before resuming their journey in the morning. Did the angels accept his offer of hospitality? (At first no, but later they did.) They said they would just spend the night in the open square, but Lot insisted that they come to his house for a meal and shelter. What did Lot prepare for his guests? (A feast and unleavened bread)

Read Genesis 19:15-16. Upon arriving at Lot's house, the angels revealed their purpose for being in Sodom. They were giving Lot and his family a warning to flee the city before God destroyed it. Sodom and Gomorrah were filled with people who had been committing great wickedness before the Lord and now it was time for judgment to take place. The Lord was going to destroy these two cities. But first, he was giving righteous Lot and his family a chance to escape. (**Read II Peter 2:6-8.**) How many children did Lot and his wife have? (Two daughters) When morning arrived, what did the two angels do? (They grabbed Lot and his wife and daughters by the hand to get them out of the city.) Lot and his family didn't seem to be in too much of a hurry, but the angels knew it was urgent to get out of Sodom quickly. (This might also serve as a good reminder to us not to linger around sin but to get away from it as quick as possible!)

Read Genesis 15:17-22. Once Lot and his family were outside the city, what instructions did the angels give them? (Escape for your lives, and do not look back.) Why do you think they were told not to look back? (Answers will vary.) We don't know why exactly, but the important thing to remember is that Lot and his family were given a very specific command from God through the message of the angels: *Do not look back.* God was being merciful in sparing Lot and his family from the destruction of the city. They needed to do their part by obeying what God was telling them to do. Where did the angels direct Lot to take his family? (To the mountains) Where did Lot ask to go instead? (Lot wanted to take his family to the little city of Zoar that was close by.) The angels agreed to Lot's request but told him to hurry.

Read Genesis 15:23-26. As soon as Lot and his family had arrived at the city of Zoar, what did the Lord do? (He rained down fire and brimstone on Sodom and Gomorrah.) While this was happening, what did Lot's wife do, and what happened to her as a result? (She looked back, and was immediately turned into a pillar of salt.) Why do you think she looked back? (Answers will vary.) Her husband was called a righteous man, but Jesus used the example of Lot's wife as a warning to others to not turn back to the things of the world. (**Luke 17:30-32.**) Lot's wife was longing for what was behind her instead of looking forward with gratefulness and obedience to the Lord for what He had done.

Read Job 1:1-3. The events of the book of Job take place around the time that Abraham lived. We learn quite a lot about Job in these first three verses. He was a very righteous man who turned away from evil and followed the Lord. He is described as *blameless and upright.* He had an excellent reputation. He was married with children. How many children did he have? (He had seven sons and three daughters.) He was also very rich! In ancient times, a person was often considered wealthy based on the size of their flocks, herds, and servants. Describe the possessions of Job. (He had 7,000 sheep, 3,000 camels, 500 yoke of oxen, and 500 female donkeys.) Now consider the amount of servants he must have had working for him to take care of so many animals! Job's wife is not mentioned until later, but first we need to learn about Job and what happened to him.

Read Job 1:8-12. Who is having a conversation in these verses? (The Lord and Satan) The Lord tells Satan that there is no one else like Job in all the earth, living so righteously and turning away from evil. Satan then asks the Lord a question about Job. What was it? ("Does Job fear God for nothing?") Satan tells the Lord that the only reason Job is such a good man is because God blesses him so much. BUT! If the Lord were to take away everything that Job had, that would be a different story! What does Satan think Job would do if that were to happen? (He thinks Job would curse God to His face.) The Lord puts Job in Satan's hands. He tells Satan that he may do what he will to everything belonging to Job, but there is one thing which he may not do. What is it? (Satan is not allowed to hurt Job physically.) Satan leaves the presence of the Lord and prepares to put a plan into action. The Lord has all power and is the one in control always. Notice that it is the Lord who gives Satan permission to test Job in this way.

Read Job 1:13-19. This must have been one of the worst days of Job's life. Can you imagine so many bad things happening all in one day? In all, there were four messengers who came to Job, delivering bad news. What did the first messenger tell Job? (He told him that the oxen and donkeys were stolen away by the Sabeans, and the servants tending the animals were killed.) He was still filling Job in on what happened when the second messenger arrived to give him the bad news that all of the sheep were burnt up. As he was speaking, the third messenger arrived to give him the bad news about the camels. What news did the last messenger bring to Job? (He told him that all of his children had been killed.) It would be bad enough to find out that all of your wealth had been wiped out in a day, but the news that all of your children had just died would be absolutely devastating. Remember, this is all Satan's doing. God gave him permission to do this to test Job, and Satan is doing this to see if he can get Job to curse God.

Read Job 1:20-22. Does Job curse God? (No!) Quite the opposite, in fact. He falls to the ground and worships. This is an amazing thing and a display of great faith and humility before God. It doesn't mean that Job doesn't care about what has happened. He was very upset and sorrowful. What are the two things he does as soon as all of the bad news has been given to him? (He tears his robe and shaves his head.) Both of these actions were signs of deep grief. Job says he was naked when he was born, and he'll be naked when he dies. What he is saying is that he came into the world with nothing, and he'll leave the world with nothing. Whom does Job say is the one who gives and takes away? (The Lord) What is the last thing Job says? ("Blessed be the name of the Lord.") Remember what Satan was trying to get Job to do? Instead of cursing God, Job is blessing the name of God. In spite of everything that he had lost that day, Job didn't become angry at God or blame Him for any of it.

Read Job 2:1-6. Satan comes back into the presence of the Lord and has another conversation with Him. Satan's first attack on Job didn't work as Satan had hoped, so he's going to try again. The Lord reminds Satan that Job is still an upright and blameless man even though Satan tried to stir him up against God. This time Satan says that Job will most certainly curse God if he suffers pain and agony in his own body. Does God give Satan permission this time to make Job suffer physically? (Yes) What one thing does the Lord not allow Satan to do to Job? (Satan is not allowed to kill Job.)

Read Job 2:7-8. How does Satan attack Job this time? (He strikes him with painful boils all over his body.) Have you ever seen a boil? It is a large red infected bump on the skin filled with pus. It's like a HUGE pimple. (Ewww! Right?) Just having one can cause a lot of misery because it is very painful. Job had a lot more than one. The Bible says he was covered with boils from the top of his head to the bottom of his feet. Can you imagine what that would feel like? There would be no comfortable position. You couldn't sit, stand or sleep without putting pressure on some of those painful sores. It would be completely miserable. What did Job do? (He sat in a pile of ashes and scraped himself with a potsherd.) A potsherd would be something like a piece of broken pottery. He sat in misery just scraping himself with it. As miserable as he is, Job still does not curse God or lash out at Him in anger or pain. It was not God that did this to him, but Job does not know that. Someone else *does* believe that God has caused all this misery. Get ready to meet Mrs. Job.

Read Job 2:9-10. Remember what Satan's goal has been through both of these attacks on Job? He wants Job to curse God. Now Job's wife is adding to her husband's misery by actually encouraging him to do such a terrible thing. She is angry. She is upset. She too has lost all of her children and a comfortable, wealthy lifestyle, and now she has a husband covered in sores. But Job still holds to his integrity. That is, he is still a righteous man who is doing what is right. He does not sin by rebelling against God. His wife, though, wants him to let go of that goodness in his heart, and let God have it! While Job is in great grief and great physical pain, his wife now tempts him to turn his back on God. How does Job answer her? (He said she was talking foolishly.) Job says something similar to what he said in chapter 1, verse 21. In that verse he said the Lord gives and takes away. In verse 10 of chapter 2, he says they should accept whatever God decides to give them, both the good and the bad. This is very remarkable. He still doesn't know that Satan is the cause of all of this misery. He thinks it has come from God, yet he is willing to accept everything God gives him. Verse 10 ends with saying that Job did not sin with his lips (his words). The Lord had told Satan that there was no one else on earth like Job. How sad that he didn't have a wife that was like him.

Read I Kings 15:1-3. Here we are introduced to our third "negative Nellie" whose name was Maacah. What are some things we learn about her from these verses? (She was the mother of Abijam, king of Judah. She was the granddaughter of Absalom.) She had been married to king Rehoboam who was Abijam's father, and her grandfather was Absalom who was one of the sons of king David. (*Note: Some versions say her grandfather was Abishalom. This is simply another name for Absalom.) Maacah was of royal blood and was placed in important positions in the kingdom of Judah. This would mean she had a great opportunity to do good and be a good influence. Sadly, this was not the case. What kind of king was her son? (He was not faithful to the Lord.)

Read I Kings 15:9-11. Abijam was no longer king because he had died. His son, Asa, now reigned in his place as the king of Judah. Maacah was his grandmother. What kind of king was Asa? (Asa was a good king who did what was right.) Asa was not like his father, Abijam.

Read I Kings 15:12-13. When Asa became king, he started to clean house! The kingdom of Judah was filled with idolatry which his father had promoted throughout the land. He removed all the idols his father had made, but unfortunately, his father's idolatry wasn't the only problem. His own grandmother, Maacah, had made and set up an idolatrous image. This was serious. Not only was it completely disobedient to the Lord, it was also dangerous because it served as an evil influence on others. What did Asa do with it? (He cut it down and burned it.) Maacah held the position of "queen mother" in the royal court of her grandson, but Asa removed her from her important position because of her blatant disobedience to the Lord. Her idolatry had no part in his kingdom. Maacah was not a good influence on her grandson or any of the people in his kingdom. She was not noble and pure but wicked and dangerous.

What do these three "Negative Nellies" teach us? Lot's wife was certainly not an encouragement to her husband in being a faithful follower of God, and she disobeyed the command from God given by the angels. Job's wife should have tried to be a comfort to her husband and encouraged him that both of them should seek the Lord and His help in their time of trial, but she discouraged that and instead tried to convince Job to completely turn away from God. Maacah was not a good grandmother! Instead of encouraging her grandson Asa to be a good king who loved the Lord, she made it harder on him to rule in that way as she promoted idolatry in the land of Judah. Discouragement is a powerful tool, and we should try hard to avoid the temptation of using it. We need to strive to be encouragers for others in the things that are good and right. Disobedience to God is dangerous. We will not always succeed in being obedient 100% of the time, but it should be our goal we work toward. **Philippians 4:8** is a beautiful reminder of how we should think and be, not just as women but as God's people: *Finally, brethren, whatever things are true, whatever things are noble, whatever things are just, whatever things are pure, whatever things are lovely, whatever things are of good report, if there is any virtue and if there is anything praiseworthy – think on these things.*

Review Questions: (Answers are provided in the Answer Key.

1. Who was Lot related to, and how were they related?

2. How many children did Lot and his wife have?

3. Once Lot and his family were outside the city of Sodom, what instructions did the angels give them?

4. Where did Lot and his family escape to?

5. What happened to Sodom and Gomorrah once Lot and his family were safely away?

6. What did Lot's wife do, and what happened to her as a result?

7. Who gave a warning in Luke 17:32 to, *"Remember Lot's wife."*?

8. What kind of man was Job spiritually?

9. How many children did Job have?

10. Describe Job's wealth.

11. What reason does Satan give the Lord for Job being such a righteous man before God?

12. What does Satan think Job will do if the Lord were to take everything away from him?

13. What does the Lord give Satan permission to do in their first conversation?

14. How many messengers brought bad news to Job?

15. What was the last bit of bad news that Job received?

16. How much of Job's possessions were lost?

17. What outward signs of grief did Job display?

18. How did Job react to the Lord after receiving all of this bad news?

19. How did Satan attack Job the second time?

20. What did Job do after this happened?

21. What did Job's wife want him to do?

22. How did Job answer her?

23. Who was Maacah's husband? Son? Grandfather?

24. What kind of king was Maacah's grandson, Asa?

25. What position did Maacah hold in Asa's royal court?

26. What did Asa do to her?

27. Why did Asa do this?

"Putting Down Roots": Memory Work

• Memorize Proverbs 25:24

• Memorize Matthew 12:30

• Memorize Philippians 4:8

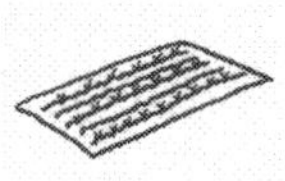

"Farther Afield": Map Work
Map 3

• Locate the city of Sodom

• Locate the city of Gomorrah

• Locate the city of Zoar

• Locate the land of Uz

• Locate the city of Jerusalem

• Locate the region of Judah

• Locate the Brook Kidron

"Harvest Fun": Games & Activities

• Scripture Puzzle Race - This race will need two players or two teams. Before the race can begin, each team will need to write out Philippians 4:8 on one sheet of construction paper. Turn the paper over and draw several random lines all over it. Then cut along the lines to make puzzle pieces. Scramble the puzzle pieces together and place them in a pile. When "Go" is called, each team will race to complete their puzzle. Whoever puts their puzzle together first wins. Read the scripture aloud and discuss which of these positive qualities were missing in our "Negative Nellies."

- "Escape from Sodom!" Obstacle Course - Your goal is to get out of Sodom and to the safety of the city of Zoar before destruction begins! To prepare, set up an obstacle course any way you would like in a back yard or very large indoor room. You can use things like pool noodle arches to crawl under, tires to jump in and out of, safety cones to zig zag around, rolling a hula hoop around wooden stakes, etc. At the finish line, place a large poster board with the name of the city of Zoar on it. The object of this activity is to successfully navigate the obstacle course in the quickest amount of time, and remembering to not look behind you as Lot's wife did!

 ## "Digging Deeper": Research

- Angels – Two angels were sent to Lot and his family in Sodom to warn them of the coming destruction. Not a lot is known about angels, but there are some things we can learn about them from scripture. Dig deep and see if you can find the answers to the following questions: 1) Are angels created beings? 2) What are some of the kinds of angels (titles or groups) talked about in the Bible? 3) Only two angels are named in scripture. Who are they? 4) Are angels supposed to be worshiped? 5) Who is the "Angel of the Lord"? 6) List each occasion in scripture that an angel(s) appeared to people either as angels or as men.

- Absalom and Asa – Maacah was the granddaughter of Absalom and the grandmother of Asa. Research and write down what you learn about the lives of these two men from the following scriptures: Absalom - II Samuel 13:22-39; II Samuel 14-15:14; II Samuel 16:15-23; II Samuel 17:1-20; II Samuel 18:9-18 Asa - I Kings 15:14-24; II Chronicles 14, 15 & 16. In what ways were these men similar? In what ways were they different?

"Food For Thought": Puzzles

- Coded Message – Use the key to break the code and read the message.

___ ___ ___ ___ ___   ___ ___ ___ ___ ___ ___ ,

17 22   8   6   8   4   26   9 13 22 23

" ___ ___ ___ ___ ___ ___ ___ ___   ___ ___ ___'___   ___ ___ ___ ___ ."

9 22 14 22 14 25 22   9   15 12   7   8   4 18 21 22

Key to the Code:

F N R U A G O S V C H T D I E B W K Y P M L J Z Q X

21 13 9 6 26 20 12 8 5 24 19 7 23 18 22 2 25 4 16 11 14 15 17 1 10 3

- Who Am I? - Read the following clues, and choose the right name. Answers are provided in the Answer Key.

Lot	Abraham	The Lord	King David
angel	Absalom	Job's wife	Lot's wife
	Maacah	Asa	

1. I was the grandfather of Maacah. _____

2. I turned into a pillar of salt. _____

3. My nephew lived in the city of Sodom. _____

4. I told my husband to curse God and die. _____

5. My son was king Abijam of Judah. _____

6. I was the grandson of Maacah who became king of Judah. _____

7. I warned Lot and his family not to look back. _____

8. Abraham was my uncle. _____

9. I rained down fired and brimstone on Sodom and Gomorrah. _____

10. Absalom was my son. _____

"Fruits Of Our Labor": Crafts

*   Salt Painting – Since Lot's wife was turned into a pillar of salt when she looked back, let's make a salt painting of her! For this craft, you will need a piece of white card stock paper, a bottle of white glue, salt, liquid watercolor paints and paintbrush. First, squeeze glue onto the card stock to "draw" your picture of Lots' wife. Next, generously sprinkle salt all over your picture until it fully covers all of the lines of glue. Tap the paper over a waste basket or into a tray to get rid of all the loose salt crystals. Dip a paintbrush into liquid watercolor paint and gently touch the salty lines on your paper. Neat, isn't it? After your picture is finished and completely dry, you may want to print the reminder Jesus gave in Luke 17:32, "Remember Lot's wife."

*   Scratch Art – Job scraped his sores with broken pottery, we're going to scrape paint to make a picture of it! For this craft you will need: a large sheet of white paper, crayons (in bright colors), black poster paint or tempera paint, dishwashing liquid, sponge brush, and toothpicks or wooden skewers. First, you will need to color the entire surface of the white paper with bright colors. Just color a block section or stripe in one color, then choose another color and color another block or stripe right next to it, etc. until there is no white paper showing. Make your colors bold and thick. Next, mix about ½ cup of paint with 1 tsp. of dishwashing

soap in a disposable cup. Use the sponge brush to cover the entire colored surface with the black paint. You may have to do more than one coat. You want a solid black picture with no crayon showing through. Let it dry completely then use a sharp tool such as a toothpick or skewer to draw a picture of Job sitting on the ashes with his wife standing by telling him to turn his back on God by scratching through the black paint. Wherever you scratch, the paint will come off and the colors will show through!

Lesson 11: The Syro-Phoenician Woman
A Woman of Persistence & Humility

Text: Matthew 15:21-28

"Growing In The Word": Lesson Text & Discussion

Read Matthew 15:21-22. Jesus had been healing many people in the land of Gennesaret (Matthew 14:34-36), but now he leaves that area and goes to the region of Tyre and Sidon. These were two major cities in the coastal country of Phoenicia. While there, a woman from that country approaches him with a very heavy heart. How does she address Jesus, and what does she ask him to do for her? (She calls him "Lord, Son of David", and she asked Him to have mercy on her.) Since Jesus is the Son of God, and Joseph was his earthly father, why does she call Jesus the "Son of David"? Jesus was a descendant of King David who reigned over Israel hundreds of years before. The promised Messiah that the Jews were looking for was to be a descendant of David. This woman is not named in scripture but is often referred to as the Syro-Phoenician woman because she came from the country of Phoenicia or what was then known as Syro-Phoenicia. She begs Jesus to have mercy on her because she has a very big problem in her life. What is it? (Her daughter was demon-possessed.) Demon possession was a terrible thing to endure. Fortunately, we do not have it today, but there were several cases of it described in the New Testament. (You will learn more about this topic in the research portion of the lesson.) A demon was a spirit under the control of Satan who would enter the body of a person. That demon would then control that person's body and cause physical pain or harm to that person. Loved ones and friends of that person would be helpless to do anything about it. Only one who had more power than the demon could heal someone who was demon-possessed. This woman loved her daughter and couldn't bear to see her suffer in such a way. She looked for and found the one person that she knew could do something about her situation. She went to Jesus and begged him to have mercy. Do you know what mercy is? (Allow responses.) Mercy is love, kindness and compassion which acts in some way to relieve suffering. It is more than just feeling sorry for someone; it is doing something kind to help them.

Read Matthew 15:23-24. How did Jesus respond to what the woman said to him? (He ignored her.) This may seem very strange and even rude. This woman comes to Jesus with a breaking heart and asks him for mercy, and he doesn't say a word to her. But Jesus has good reasons for what he is doing. Who else is with Jesus and this woman? (The disciples of Jesus) What did the disciples want Jesus to do? (They wanted him to send her away.) They seem to be annoyed by her and don't want to be bothered. Maybe they just want her to go away, or maybe they want Jesus to just hurry up and do what she wants so she'll leave them alone. Either way, they tell Jesus to just get rid of her! How does Jesus respond to this? (He says he was sent only to the Israelites.) Jesus is saying that he was sent to the Jews (the house of Israel). This woman is not a Jew but a Canaanite woman. Anyone who was not a Jew was called a Gentile. Jesus is saying he was sent to help those who were Jews, not Gentiles. So, he is basically telling this woman, "I can't help you because you're not a Jew!" This may also seem strange and rude for him to say, but Jesus knows this woman's heart. He knows how far she will go to seek help for her daughter, and he also knows that his disciples are watching and listening to all of this take place. This does not mean that Jesus did not love the Gentile people, but his purpose was to minister to the Jews. Later on when the church began, the gospel was to be preached to every person in the world, both Jews and Gentiles. God truly loves everyone.

Read Matthew 15:25. No matter what Jesus has done and said so far, this woman does not give up. That is what it persistence is – not giving up. Now she does something extraordinary. What is it? (She worships Jesus.) Instead of being insulted or stomping off angrily or with hurt feelings, she worships Jesus. To worship means to show reverence, and give honor, praise and glory. This woman has already called Jesus "Lord, Son of David", and now she worships him as God. She has an incredibly strong faith that believes in who he is, and that he is the only one with the power to help her. What does she cry out to him this time? ("Lord, help me!") She knows there is no one else to whom she can go for help, so she begs him for his.

Read Matthew 15:26-27. Jesus' answer to her second plea for help might seem strange. He talks about not taking bread away from the children to throw to the little dogs. The Jews were called the children of God, and many of them looked down on the Gentile people and would even refer to them as dogs. Jesus is again emphasizing the difference between them – he is a Jew and she is a Gentile. He's asking her if it is right for him to take what blessings he should be giving his own people (the Jews) and throwing them away on dogs (Gentiles) like her. You may be thinking by now that Jesus is being really mean to this woman. Isn't he supposed to love and help everyone? Remember that Jesus never sinned; he was perfect in everything that he did. He sees this woman's heart, and he knows "how much she can take." He knows she is a woman of great faith, persistence and humility. He is giving her a test, and so far, she is passing it. She admits that what Jesus said is true. She's acknowledging that she doesn't deserve anything, but is asking for just a little from him. What does she ask for? (Crumbs) She says that even the little dogs will eat any crumbs they can get that may fall from the table, and that is all she is asking for. Not only has the woman shown great persistence, (remember what that means?) but she also shows great humility. Humility is thinking of others before yourself.

It is the opposite of pride. If this woman were full of pride, she would have been angry and insulted by the words of Jesus. She might have even angrily demanded, "How dare you!" But that isn't her attitude at all. She isn't thinking of herself or her feelings at this time. Who do you think she is thinking of? (Allow answers.) She is thinking about her poor daughter who needs help, and she is willing to plead with Jesus and patiently take whatever he tells her for as long as is needed until she gets what she wants – healing for her precious daughter.

Read Matthew 15:28. At last! Jesus finally gives this woman the greatest desire of her heart. First, he praises her. This foreign woman, this Gentile, is praised by Jesus. What does he praise her for? (He praises her great faith.) Remember, the disciples of Jesus were here too, and they had wanted him to send her away. They had heard the words Jesus spoke to her and seen her persistence and humility and faith through it all. What a great lesson for them to see a Gentile woman have so much faith and reverence for the Son of God. Because of this woman's strong faith and humble attitude, Jesus gives her exactly what she wants. When did he heal her daughter? (At that very hour) Can you imagine how happy this mother would have been to arrive home and find her daughter completely healed from a horrible demon possession? If you could ask her if she would go through it all again, or if it was worth it, what do you think she would say?

This Syro-Phoenician woman teaches us how important it is to be persistent in asking the Lord for help for the things we struggle with. When we need help from the Lord, we can go to Him in prayer over and over asking, "Lord, help me!" She also shows us what a heart of humility looks. She didn't get all bent out of shape or get her feelings hurt over the first few responses of Jesus. It wasn't about her; it was about what her daughter needed. She believed in Jesus and what he could do for her and her daughter, so she never gave up being reverent and having faith. She fits the description of faith that we read in **Hebrews 11:6,** *But without faith it is impossible to please Him, for he who comes to God must believe that He is, and that He is a rewarder of those who diligently seek Him.*

Review Questions: (Answers are provided in the Answer Key.)

1. How did the Syro-Phoenician woman refer to Jesus?

2. What was wrong with this woman's daughter?

3. What was Jesus' first response to her?

4. What did the disciples ask Jesus to do and why?

5. To whom did Jesus say he was sent?

6. This woman was not a Jew. What group would she be in as a non-Jew?

7. What does persistence mean?

8. After being told that he was only sent to the Jews, what did the woman do next?

9. After pleading for his help again, how did Jesus answer her?

10. Did the woman take his answer as an insult?

11. What does humility mean?

12. The woman admitted that what Jesus said was true, but what did she still ask for?

13. What did Jesus praise her for?

14. Jesus gave her the desire of her heart. What was it?

15. When did he do this?

 "Putting Down Roots": Memory Work

- Memorize Matthew 15:28

- Memorize Hebrews 11:6

 "Farther Afield": Map Work
   Map 5

- Locate the city of Tyre

- Locate the city of Sidon

- Locate the region of Phoenicia

- Locate the country of Syria

"Harvest Fun": Games & Activities

- Proud or Humble? – Open up your Bibles as fast as you can to each location as it is called out. Whoever finds the scripture first needs to read it out loud, identify the person the verses are talking about, and whether that person was proud or humble in that circumstance. If you don't want to use this activity as a race, simply assign different passages to the participants, then continue with the instructions above. Remember that humility thinks of others above yourself just as the Syro-Phoenician woman demonstrated in our lesson.

    Scriptures:

    I Kings 21:29   (Ahab – humble)

    Mark 1:6-7   (John the Baptist – humble)

    Daniel 5:22-23   (Belshazzar – proud)

    Philippians 2:8   (Jesus – humble)

    Acts 12:21-23   (Herod – proud)

    Exodus 5:2   (Pharaoh – proud)

    Esther 5:11-12   (Haman – proud)

    Genesis 18:27   (Abraham – humble)

    II Corinthians 10:1   (Paul – humble)

    II Chronicles 33:12-13   (Manasseh – humble)

    Acts 8:9   (Simon the Sorcerer – proud)

    I Samuel 15:16-19   (Saul – proud)

    Exodus 3:11   (Moses – humble)

    II Chronicles 26:14-16   (Uzziah – proud)

- Don't Give Up! - This is a brainstorming activity, so put on your thinking caps! Think of some prayer requests you've made to God but maybe have not seen any answer. How many times have you prayed about each one? Have you shown persistence? Make a list of these requests, and add any new ones you may have. Read the following scriptures about persistence in prayer, then choose your favorite one, and write it at the bottom of your list to remind you to be persistent in going to God in prayer. Scriptures: Matthew 7:7-11; Luke 11:9-10; I Thessalonians 5:17; Psalm 88:1; Hebrews 4:16

 ## "Digging Deeper": Research

- Phoenicia – The mother in this lesson came from the region of Phoenicia, a coastal country located on the eastern side of the Mediterranean Sea. Tyre and Sidon were two of its major cities. Research this fascinating country and answer the following questions: 1) What were some of the things the ancient Phoenicians were well-known for? 2) What unique product did the Phoenicians manufacture? 3) How was it made, and what was it used for? 4) What was unique about the city of Tyre? 5) Who ultimately conquered Tyre, and how was it done?

- Demon Possession study – The Syro-Phoenician woman's daughter was not the only one to suffer from being demon possessed. Read the listed passages about demon possession, then answer the following questions: Matthew 9:32-34; Matthew 12:22-30; Matthew 17:14-21; Mark 1:23-26; Mark 9:38-41; Luke 8:26-39; Luke 9:1; Acts 16:16-18; Acts 19:11-17. 1) Describe who could be possessed by a demon (Male or female? Old or young?) 2) What were some of the things demons caused the people they possessed to do? 3) List all of those who were authorized (and successful) at casting out demons. 4) List any who were not successful at casting out demons because they did not have authority from God to do so. 5) What were the reactions of witnesses to each of these accounts? 6) Demons are under the authority and power of Satan, but whom did they obey in each of these accounts?

Each of these accounts of demon-possession show how powerful Satan and his demons were, but they also show that the Lord has all power and has authority to command the demons.

"Food For Thought": Puzzles

- Sequence – Put the events of this lesson in the correct order, numbering them from 1-10. Answers are provided in the Answer Key.

_____ 1. The Syro-Phoenician woman told Jesus that even dogs eat the crumbs that fall from their master's table.

_____2. Jesus did not answer her a word.

_____3. Her daughter was healed from that very hour.

_____4. Jesus went to the region of Tyre and Sidon.

_____5. She came and worshiped Him.

_____6. She told Jesus that her daughter was severely demon-possessed.

_____7. She said to Jesus, "Lord, help me!"

_____8. The disciples urged Jesus to send her away.

_____9. Jesus told the woman that it wasn't good to take the children's bread and throw it to the dogs.

_____10. Jesus praised the woman for her great faith.

- Finish the Verse – Complete the following verses which were contained in this lesson. All quotations are taken from the NKJV. Answers are provided in the Answer Key.

1. "Then she came and worshiped Him, saying, '_____.'" (Matthew 15:25)

2. "And behold, a woman of Canaan, came from that region and cried out to Him, saying, 'Have mercy on me, O Lord, Son of David! My _____

_____.'"

(Matthew 15:22)

3. "Jesus answered and said to her, 'O woman, _____

_____

And her daughter was healed from that very hour." (Matthew 15:28)

4. "And His disciples came and urged Him, saying, '_____

_____.'"

(Matthew 15:23)

5. "And she said, 'True, Lord, yet even the little dogs _____

_____.'"

(Matthew 15:27)

"Fruits Of Our Labor": Crafts

• Tie-Dye – The Syro-Phoenician woman came from a country that was well-known for manufacturing purple dye. Try your hand at dyeing a shirt purple! For this craft you will need: a white cotton T-shirt, RIT purple dye (available at most craft stores and some grocery stores), trash bags, old containers to mix the dye, disposable gloves, and rubber bands or string. A day or two before your start, pre-wash your T-shirt to make sure it's clean and won't shrink. When you're ready to dye, carefully read the instructions that came with your dye and follow the mixing steps. Always wear your gloves when mixing and working with the dye. Prepare a large work surface by covering it with plastic trash bags. These can be taped down to prevent sliding. Lay your clean, dry T-shirt on the plastic and begin tying. You can use rubber bands or string to secure each spot you tie. Be creative! You can make a spiral, a bulls-eye of circles, stripes, or random circles all over. Just pull up a "bump" of shirt and tie it off with the rubber band or string.

Remember that everywhere you have a rubber band will be white or light when the bands are removed later. When your shirt is all tied as you'd like, dye it purple according to the directions. Let it dry according to the directions and make sure you clean up and dispose of the dye as you should. Remove your bands and...Ta-da! You now have a purple-dyed shirt! And your dye was much easier to make and use than what the Phoenicians had back in Bible times. Did you know that purple dye in ancient times was made from a type of snail? Aren't you glad your dye came in a box? As you wear your purple shirt, remember the great faith of the Syro-Phoenician woman.

• Bookmark - Cut white card stock 2 inches wide by 6 inches long. Copy the verse, "But without faith it is impossible to please Him, for he who comes to God must believe that He is, and that He is a rewarder of those who diligently seek Him." -Hebrews 11:6 on it. You may want to try calligraphy or other fancy hand-writing. Draw a decorative border around it or decorate any way you choose. When finished, laminate your bookmark or cover it with contact paper. If you'd like, punch a hole near the top and tie a pretty ribbon through it.

Lesson 12: Priscilla & Sapphira
A Wise Wife & A Worldly Wife

Text: Acts 5:1-11; 18:1-3, 24-26; Romans 16:3-5

"Growing In The Word": Lesson Text & Discussion

In this lesson, we'll look at two married women who were very different from each other. Both of them "helped" their husbands, but only one helped in the right way and for a right reason.

Read Acts 5:1-2. Here we are introduced to a married couple named Ananias and Sapphira. They sold something that they owned which we later read was a piece of land. They were doing this in order to contribute money to the church. If you look back at the last two verses of chapter 4, you will see that others did this as well. We read that Barnabas sold his land and brought the money to the apostles at the church. Ananias and Sapphira seemed to be doing the same thing, but it was not. Were they going to give all the money they received for the sale of their land? (No) Ananias decided to keep back part of the money for themselves, and his wife Sapphira knew it and went right along with his plan. He went alone, taking the money and laying it at the feet of the apostles.

Read Acts 5:3-4. Which apostle spoke to Ananias? (Peter) Peter did not thank Ananias for his generous contribution, but instead, accused him of a sin. What sin did he say Ananias had committed? (Lying) Ananias had lied about the amount of money he sold the land for. Apparently, Peter had asked him if the amount given was the amount the land sold for and Ananias had said that it was. This was not true. Was it wrong for Ananias and Sapphira to keep part of the money for themselves? (No) Peter told Ananias that when he sold the land, the money was his to do with whatever he liked. If he wanted to donate all of it to the church, great. If he only wanted to donate part of it and use the rest to remodel his house, pay bills, or whatever, that was fine too. The problem and sin was in the fact that he lied to Peter and the rest of the apostles by saying he had given all of it. Peter was not as concerned with the fact that Ananias had lied to *him*, but he was very concerned about who Ananias was really lying to. Who did Peter accuse him of lying to? (The Holy Spirit) Who did Peter say had put that into the heart of Ananias? (Satan) **John 8:44** tells us that Satan is a liar and the father of lies. Lying to the Holy Spirit, to God is a serious matter. **Proverbs 6:17** tells us that the Lord hates a lying tongue.

Read Acts 5:5-6. What happened as soon as Ananias heard the words of Peter? (He fell down dead at Peter's feet.) People who were there at the time started spreading the word of what had happened. How did it affect the people who heard about it? (They were afraid.) What was done to the body of Ananias? (It was carried out and buried.) Meanwhile, Sapphira was still home, waiting for Ananias to return, but he didn't.

Read Acts 5:7-9. Three hours later, and Ananias still hadn't returned home. Sapphira wanted to know what had happened, so she went to see the apostles. Peter questioned her about the sale of their land. He asked her if they had sold it for a certain amount (the amount that Ananias had brought as a contribution.) Sapphira was faced with a choice: Would she tell the truth to the apostles and before God, or would she stick with her husband and tell the lie? What choice did she make? (She lied.) Peter was amazed that she would agree to do such a thing with her husband. It is great for wives to support their husbands but not when it is to do something that is wrong. In that case, she should stand alone if necessary to do what is right. Sapphira, like her husband, was worldly. They wanted to look good and appear so generous in front of everybody by saying they had sold their land and donated all of the money to the church, but they also wanted to keep some money for themselves to spend as they wished. They were more concerned with themselves and what they wanted than being concerned with helping others. Pride, greediness, and worldliness have no place in the heart of a Christian.

Read Acts 5:10-11. What happened to Sapphira as soon as she lied to Peter? (She fell down dead at his feet.) She was carried out and buried right next to her husband. They agreed to lie together in life, and it cost them both their lives so they will lie next to each other in death. How sad! What if Sapphira had tried to influence her husband to do right? What if she had talked to him, encouraging him to be a strong Christian by telling the truth and putting the needs of others before themselves? We will never know. Sapphira helped her husband in the wrong way. She made the choice to do evil right along with him instead of doing what was right.

Now let's look at the example of another woman who stood with her husband but helped him to do what was right.

Read Acts 18:1-3. The apostle Paul had traveled to the city of Corinth, and he met a Christian couple who worked in the same trade as he. What were their names? (Aquila and Priscilla) They were tent-makers as was Paul, so he stayed with them and worked with them to earn his living while being in Corinth to preach. We're not told too much about Aquila and Priscilla here other than they were Jews who had just moved to Corinth from Italy and were tent-makers who let Paul work and live with them. Let's read on to learn more.

Read Acts 18:24-26. Here we read about a man named Apollos who was preaching and teaching in the city of Ephesus. He was very enthusiastic about preaching the gospel, and he was teaching the truth, but there was still a problem. What was it? (He only knew of the baptism of John.) While he was alive, John the baptist had been preaching repentance to the people and encouraging them to be baptized for repentance. Read **Acts 19:4.** After Jesus had died on the cross and was resurrected, and after his church was established on the day of Pentecost, baptism changed. According to **Acts 2:38**, whose name was one to be baptized in, and what was the baptism for? (For those who believe that Jesus is the Christ, the Son of God, baptism is to be done in his name for the remission of sins.) Priscilla and her husband heard the preaching of Apollos and wanted to help him learn about baptism in the name of Jesus Christ. Did they call him out in front of everyone and embarrass him publicly, or did they teach him privately? (They took him aside and taught him privately.) Priscilla was helping her husband teach another person how to do right. What a difference from Sapphira who helped her husband do what was wrong.

Read Romans 16:3-5. We learn even more about Priscilla and her husband in these verses. First of all, how does Paul refer to them? (Fellow workers in Christ Jesus) They were faithful Christians who worked hard in the church and helped others in any way they could. They even helped Paul in some memorable way because he says they *"risked their own necks for my life"*. Paul was often threatened when he preached Jesus. Sometimes, he was thrown in prison, beaten, or even stoned. There must have been an occasion when he was in trouble of some sort like this, and Aquila and Priscilla helped him at a great risk to their own safety. What faithful friends! We also learn from these verses that a church met in their home. House churches were very common in the first century.

In all of these verses, Priscilla is listed as diligently working right alongside her husband whether it was in their tent-making trade, teaching the gospel, helping others, or showing hospitality by opening their home for a church to meet there. Sapphira and Priscilla were married women who worked together with their husbands but definitely not in the same way. Sapphira was the worldly wife who joined her husband in doing wrong while Priscilla shines as a bright example of a wise wife who helped her husband work for the Lord. **Proverbs 12:4** tells us, *"An excellent wife is the crown of her husband."* Priscilla could certainly be called Aquila's crown!

Review Questions: (Answers are provided in the Answer Key.)

1. What did Ananias and Sapphira sell?

2. What did they decide to do with the money from the sale?

3. What sin did Peter accuse Ananias of?

4. Was it wrong of Ananias and Sapphira to keep back part of the money from their sale?

5. Who did Peter say had put this sin into the heart of Ananias?

6. Who does John 8:44 refer to as "*the father of lies*"?

7. What happened to Ananias as a result of his sin?

8. Did Sapphira know what had happened to her husband?

9. How long was it from the time Ananias went to Peter and the time Sapphira went to him?

10. Did Sapphira have a chance to do what was right?

11. What choice did she make, and what was the result?

12. Where was Sapphira buried?

13. What was the name of Priscilla's husband?

14. What trade did she and her husband work at?

15. Which apostle came to work and live with them for awhile?

16. Who did Priscilla and her husband teach privately?

17. How did Paul describe Priscilla and her husband in Romans 16?

18. In what way had Priscilla and her husband helped Paul?

19. What group met in the home of Priscilla and her husband?

20. Priscilla shows us an example of an excellent wife. How does Proverbs 12:4 describe a wife such as that?

"Putting Down Roots": Memory Work

- Memorize Proverbs 12:4

- Memorize Acts 5:9

"Farther Afield": Map Work
Map 6

- Locate the city of Rome

- Locate the country of Italy

- Locate the region of Pontus

- Locate the city of Alexandria

- Locate the city of Ephesus

"Harvest Fun": Games & Activities

- Which Woman? - For this game, each player will need two index cards. On one card, write the name "Priscilla", and on the other write the name "Sapphira". As the following clues are read aloud, each player will hold up the card containing the correct answer.

1. This woman had a conversation with the apostle Peter. (Sapphira)

2. This woman's husband was Aquila. (Priscilla)

3. The apostle Paul worked and stayed with this woman and her husband. (Priscilla)

4. This woman had lived in Italy. (Priscilla)

5. This woman's husband was Ananias. (Sapphira)

6. This woman was buried by her husband. (Sapphira)

7. This woman helped her husband teach Apollos. (Priscilla)

8. This woman risked her neck for the apostle Paul. (Priscilla)

9. A church met in the house of this woman. (Priscilla)

10. This woman conspired with her husband to lie to God. (Sapphira)

11. This woman's death brought great fear upon the church. (Sapphira)

12. This woman was a member of the church. (Both!)

13. This woman was a tentmaker. (Priscilla)

14. This woman's husband sold some land. (Sapphira)

15. Which woman helped her husband? (Trick question! - You could technically say both because Sapphira "helped" Ananias even though it was in wrongdoing, or you could just say Priscilla who was the godly helper to her husband.)

- For this game, players will take turns drawing while other players try to guess what the picture is. A point may be awarded for each correct picture guess. After correctly identifying a picture, another point may be awarded if the player can then explain how that particular item relates to the lesson. (Answers are provided below after each word in bold type.) Before play begins, have someone who is not playing the game write the following bold words on a card, one word per card: **land** (Ananias and Sapphira sold some land), **money** (Ananias brought money to the apostles), **feet** (Ananias laid the money at the feet of the apostles), **the church** (great fear came upon the church after Ananias and Sapphira died), **Italy** (Aquila and Priscilla had lived there), **tents** (Aquila, Priscilla, and Paul were all tent-makers), **baptism** (Apollos only knew of the baptism of John), **synagogue** (Apollos was speaking boldly here), **the Scriptures** (Apollos was described as being mighty in the Scriptures), **house** (Aquila and Priscilla held worship services in their house), **neck** (Aquila and Priscilla risked their necks for Paul). To begin playing, show one player a word card then let him have two minutes to try to draw it on either a large sheet of paper or a white board. Whichever player guesses correctly scores one point as stated above, then is given the opportunity to score an additional point by being able to explain how that item fits into the lesson. That player gets to draw next and so on until all cards are used. Player with the most points wins or this can simply be played for fun and review purposes.

"Digging Deeper": Research

- Tent-making – Aquila and Priscilla, along with the apostle Paul, were tent-makers by trade. Learn about the process of tent-making in Bible times. What materials were used? How were tents enlarged? How often would someone acquire a new tent?

- The Church – Ananias, Sapphira, Aquila, and Priscilla were all Christians in the early church. Let's research more about it and how it started. How many churches did Jesus say he would build? (Matthew 16:18) On what day was the first sermon preached and people were saved? (Acts 2:1, 40-41) How were the people saved? (Acts 2:38; 41) Who adds people to the Lord's church? (Acts 2:47) Jesus said in John 4:24 that people needed to worship God in *"spirit and in truth"*. What acts of worship do we find in the New Testament that were practiced by the Lord's church? 1. _____ (Eph. 5:19; Col. 3:16) 2. _____ (I Tim. 2:1-8) 3. _____ (I Cor. 16:1-2; II Cor. 9:7) 4. _____ (II Tim. 4:2; Acts 20:7) 5. _____ (Acts 20:7; I Cor. 11:23-29) Answers are provided in the Answer Key.

"Food For Thought": Puzzles

- "Husbands and Wives" Matching – On the following page, match the husband on the left with his wife on the right. Scriptures are provided if you need a little help. Answers are provided in the Answer Key.

Genesis 24:67	Genesis 41:45	Exodus 2:21	Ruth 1:2
Esther 2:16-17	Hosea 1:3	Matthew 1:5	Acts 5:1
	Acts 18:2	Acts 24:24	

_____ 1. Aquila   a. Sapphira

_____ 2. Moses   b. Rebekah

_____ 3. Salmon   c. Naomi

_____ 4. Joseph   d. Drusilla

_____ 5. Ananias   e. Priscilla

_____ 6. Isaac   f. Gomer

_____ 7. Ahasuerus   g. Zipporah

_____ 8. Elimilech   h. Rahab

_____ 9. Hosea   i. Asenath

_____ 10. Felix   j. Esther

- What Happened Next? - Read the following then fill in the blank with what happened next. Scriptures are listed to help you. Answers are provided in the Answer Key.

1. "Then immediately she fell down at his feet..." _____
_____ (Acts 5:10)

2. "When Aquila and Priscilla heard him..." _____
_____ (Acts 18:26)

3. "To whom not only I give thanks..." _____
_____ (Romans 16:4)

4. "Ananias, with Sapphira his wife, sold a possession..." _____

_____ (Acts 5:1-2)

5. "And the young men came in and found her dead..." _____

_____ (Acts 5:10)

6. "So great fear came upon the church..." _____

_____ (Acts 5:11)

7. "Then Ananias, hearing these words..." _____

_____ (Acts 5:5)

8. "So because he was of the same trade..." _____

_____ (Acts 18:3)

9. "He spoke and taught accurately the things of the Lord..." _____

_____ (Acts 18:25)

10. "So great fear came upon all those who heard these things..." _____

_____ (Acts 5:5-6)

"Fruits Of Our Labor": Crafts

• Tent treats – Aquila and Priscilla were skilled in the art of tent-making and used it to support themselves. Here's a tasty tent treat that makes a great snack for this lesson. After all, learning is hard work! For this snack you will need graham crackers, peanut butter or frosting, chocolate chips and fruit roll-ups or caramel wraps. First, melt some chocolate chips until smooth. Spread melted chocolate on two of the graham crackers and chill until firm. To make an A-frame tent, lay one plain cracker flat on the table for the base, and "glue" the other two chocolate-covered crackers to the base with peanut butter or frosting, chocolate side facing out. Then "glue" them together at the top, forming an upside down V. Cut a tent fly or tent flaps out of fruit roll-ups or caramel wraps to cover the back and front of the tent. You can also cover the sides of the tent with either of these in place of the chocolate if you'd like.

- Priscilla/Sapphira Paper Dolls – Use the template in Appendix B, printing out two copies. Color them and cut them out leaving a border around them so you have two matching rectangle shapes with the woman in the middle. You want to leave enough of a border so you can write words around each woman. After you've cut them out, write their name above their head, then list characteristics of each one all around them. For example, for Priscilla, you might list things like wise, helpful, honest, faithful Christian, etc. while for Sapphira you might list things like worldly, dishonest, disobedient to the Lord, etc. After you've listed characteristics for each of them, glue them back to back with a large tongue depressor between them so you have a "handle" to hold and flip the pictures back and forth. Show the finished product to someone and explain what kind of women each of them were and what kind of woman/wife God desires women to be.

Lesson 13: Dorcas

A Woman of Loving Service

Text: Acts 9:36-42

"Growing In The Word": Lesson Text & Discussion

Read Acts 9:36. Along with the word "saints", we also see Christians frequently called "disciples." A disciple is simply a follower or student so if you're a disciple of Christ, you are a follower of Christ. In this verse, we read about a certain disciple named Tabitha. Where did she live? (Joppa) The name Tabitha means "gazelle." She was also known by another name. What was it? (Dorcas) Dorcas was the Greek translation of her name and the one you may be more familiar with. We don't have any written record of anything she said, but the Bible does describe what kind of woman she was. What was she like? (A woman who did many good works and charitable deeds.) She was kind, loving, giving and compassionate. She was a woman who put her faith into action by the many good works which she did.

Read Acts 9:37-38. What happened to Dorcas? (She became sick and died.) Where was her body laid? (In an upper room) The town of Joppa where Dorcas lived was near the town of Lydda where Peter was currently staying. Who sent men to fetch Peter? (Disciples) These men were on a mission! We see they had a sense of urgency because they weren't going to dilly-dally but were going to beg Peter to come as quickly as he could. Since Dorcas was already dead, why do you think the disciples wanted Peter to come so quickly or even at all? (Answers will vary.)

Read Acts 9:39. Peter came to Joppa immediately and entered the house where Dorcas was. Who did he find there, and what were they doing? (There were some widows there weeping.) Widows are women whose husbands have died. In Bible times, widows usually had a very difficult time because they were very poor. There were no social security checks or food stamps, and it was very difficult for many of them to make enough money to provide for their needs, or to even work at all. If they had grown children, it was their responsibility to take care of them, but some widows had no one to help them. God had provided help for widows under the Law of Moses. (You will learn more about this in the research portion of this lesson.) God cared very much for widows, and He wanted His people to be caring and compassionate toward them as well. When Peter entered the house where Dorcas lay, what did the widows show to him? (The tunics and garments that Dorcas had made for them.) Here is an example of some of the good works that Dorcas did. She had sewn clothing for these widows who were probably poor and in need. Her kind and loving heart had made a huge impact on these widows as we see how sorrowful they were over her death. This is a great example to us of how we can use the talents that God gives us to help others and show God's love to them. This also shows us that Dorcas had a generous heart. She would have been obtaining the material to make the clothes at her own expense, and she would have devoted a great amount of her personal time to sew each piece of clothing by hand.

Read Acts 9:40-42. Peter made everyone leave the room where Dorcas was, then he knelt down beside her bed. What did he do next? (He prayed.) What did Peter say to Dorcas? ("Tabitha, arise.") As soon as Peter spoke, Dorcas opened her eyes and sat up! Peter, through the power of Jesus Christ, had just raised Dorcas from the dead! He took her by the hand and helped her up. Who did Peter then call? (The widows and saints) Remember that "saints" is another term for Christians, so these were Dorcas' brothers and sisters in Christ. Peter showed them that Dorcas was alive. Can you imagine what they must have thought and how they must have felt? If you had been there, what would your reaction have been? The people in this house were not the only ones who knew what the apostle Peter had done. What was the result of this miracle on the people of Joppa? (Many believed on the Lord)

These are just a few verses recorded in scripture about the woman we know as Dorcas. We don't have a record of any words she said, but we learn so much from her actions. This woman of the Bible teaches us what loving service looks like. She is described as being *"full of good works."* If a glass is full of something, such as milk, there is no room in it for anything else like soda or water. Dorcas was so full of serving others, there was no room for anything else in her life. Loving service *was* her life.

Review Questions: (Answers are provided in the Answer Key.)

1. What city did Tabitha live in?

2. What was Tabitha's other name?

3. What does the name "Tabitha" mean?

4. What kind of woman was she?

5. What happened to Tabitha?

6. Where was her body laid?

7. Who sent for Peter?

8. Were they content to let Peter come whenever he was available?

9. Who was in Tabitha's house weeping when Peter arrived?

10. What had Tabitha made for them?

11. After Peter knelt by Tabitha's bed and prayed, what did he say to her?

12. To whom did Peter show Tabitha after raising her from the dead?

13. What was the result of that miracle on the people in Joppa?

14. Do we have any record of Tabitha's words?

15. What does this woman of the Bible teach us?

 "Putting Down Roots": Memory Work

- Memorize Acts 9:36

- Memorize the 12 apostles: Peter, Andrew, James, John, Philip, Thomas, Matthew, Bartholomew, James the less, Simon, Thaddeus, Judas

 **"Farther Afield": Map Work**

Map 4

- Locate the city of Joppa

- Locate the city of Lydda

- Locate the city of Sharon

- Locate the region of Judea

"Harvest Fun": Games & Activities

- Use Your Talents! - Dorcas was a good seamstress and used that talent to make clothes for people who needed them. God has also blessed you with specific talents and abilities that you can use to help others. For example, are you good at drawing or painting? You could make some fabulous cards to send to someone who is sick or artwork to hang on someone's refrigerator to cheer them up. Do you like to bake? Great! Bake some cookies or homemade bread for someone who is hungry or recovering from an illness or surgery. Maybe you like to sew like Dorcas and can make potholders, pillow cases or Christmas stockings. Perhaps you're a good reader and could read the Bible to a shut-in or someone who doesn't have good eyesight. Not sure what your talent is? Can you work hard? Maybe your parents, grandparents, or neighbor could use some help with some yard work or household chores. Take some time to think about what you can do for others then put it into practice this week.

- Clothing Closet – Sometimes, people have a difficult time affording clothes and shoes. Some churches provide a clothing closet for this need. A small classroom can be used for this; it is just important that items stay neatly sorted so people can locate what they need quickly. If you have something like this at your congregation, consider volunteering to work in it, either by helping people who come to pick up clothes, or by helping to clean and organize the room. If your congregation doesn't have something like this, perhaps you could set something like this up with the approval of the elders or men of the congregation. Some days/times to consider when there is a greater need are back-to-school and winter.

- "I'm Thinking of a Bible Character" - This is a fun game that can be used to review all of the lessons in this book. To play this game, one player will think of a character from any of the lessons covered in this book and then say "ready." The other players will take turns asking questions that can be answered "yes" or "no" by the person who has the character. Whoever guesses correctly, gets to think of the next Bible character and play begins again. For example, I might think of the character Athaliah. Other players might ask me questions such as, "Is your person a woman?" "Yes" "Is your person in the Old Testament?" "Yes" "Was this woman a good woman?" "No" "Was she married?" "Yes" "Was it Lot's wife?" "No" "Was she a bad grandmother?" "Yes" "Is it Athaliah?" "Yes" Whoever guessed that it was Athaliah would then get to pick a Bible character and the game would continue.

 ## "Digging Deeper": Research

- Widows in the Bible – What was it like to be a widow in Bible times? How would they be supported? What provisions did the Lord make in the Law of Moses for widows to have food? (See Exodus 22:22-24; Deuteronomy 24:17-21, 26:12-13) Who were some notable widows mentioned in the Bible?

- Biblical Clothing – Dorcas had made tunics and other garments for the widows. What kinds of garments would these be? What were some different materials clothes were made out of? How were the garments made? How did the clothing of the men and women differ?

"Food For Thought": Puzzles

- Word Scramble with Clues - Read the following clues to help you unscramble the letters to form the correct answer, then write it on the line. Answers are provided in the Answer Key.

1. s i n u c t - A type of clothing _____

2. p i d c l i s e - A follower _____

3. s i w o w d – Women whose husbands have died _____

4. p e g n i w e – A synonym for crying _____

5. b a t i h a t – Means "gazelle" _____

6. a p o j p – City where Dorcas lived _____

7. t a n s i s – Another name for Christians _____

8. d a y l d - City where Peter was sent from _____

9. r t e p e – Apostle who came to Dorcas _____

10. r e d p y a – What Peter did when Dorcas had died _____

- What's Missing? - Read the following verses found in Acts 9:36-42. Choose the missing words from the box below and write them on the lines. (Quotations are taken from the NKJV.) Answers are provided in the Answer Key.

charitable	Lydda	weeping	believed	good
prayed	disciple	sick	Tabitha	saints
lifted	alive	washed	Peter	hand
upper	woman	widows	died	Lord
Dorcas	Joppa			

1. But Peter put them all out, and knelt down and _____.

2. Since _____ was near _____ and the disciples heard that _____ was there, they sent two men to him.

3. All the _____ stood by him _____.

4. At Joppa, there was a certain _____ named _____, which is translated _____.

5. When he had called the _____ and widows, he presented her _____.

6. Then he gave her his _____ and _____ her up.

7. When they had _____ her, they laid her in an _____ room.

8. This _____ was full of _____ works and _____ deeds.

9. It happened in those days that she became _____ and _____.

10. It became known throughout all Joppa, and many _____ on the _____.

"Fruits Of Our Labor": Crafts

- Sew a Felt Heart – For this project you will need the heart templates from Appendix B and two different colors of felt such as red and pink. Cut out the templates, and pin each one to a piece of felt. Trace and cut out the felt hearts. Pin the smaller heart in the center of the larger heart to hold in place while you sew. Thread a blunt-tipped embroidery needle with two strands of embroidery thread. Knot the ends. Place the needle between the edges of the two hearts and bring the needle up about $\frac{1}{4}$ inch in from the edge of the smaller heart, hiding the knot in between the two hearts. Begin sewing the hearts together by an up and down motion of stitching all around the edge of the smaller heart keeping the stitching about $\frac{1}{4}$ inch in from the edge. When finished, tie a small bow out of pretty ribbon and glue onto the larger heart just above the center of the smaller heart. If you want to display a message on the heart, you can use a fabric marker to print a message such as "I love you" and then outline it with embroidery thread before sewing the two hearts together. Give the heart to a widow who could use some cheering up or to someone you would like to give a gift to.

- Button Sewing – Some guys may not want to sew a heart and that's okay, but all guys should know how to do some sewing 101 for emergencies, such as sewing on a missing button. Help out your brother or your dad by sewing on a missing button to a shirt or pair of pants. Trust me, it's good practice! Match the thread color to what is used in the other buttons or to the color of the fabric. Carefully thread a needle and knot the end. Position the button in the right spot and bring the needle up from underneath the fabric through a hole in the button. Continue bringing the needle straight up until the thread is tight. Place the needle in the hole that is diagonal to the one you just brought the needle up through and push the needle down, pulling the thread underneath until tight. Bring the needle back up through the first hole and continue the diagonal stitch several times. Then bring the needle up through an opposite hole and start doing the same diagonal stitch in the opposite direction. You are sewing the button on by making an "X" with your thread. Once the button is secure, make sure your final stitch leaves the needle and thread underneath the fabric. Tie the thread securely in a knot and trim with the scissors.

Answer

Key

Answer Key

Lesson 1:

Review Questions:

1. On what day was Eve created? (Day 6)

2. Describe how God created Eve. (God caused a deep sleep to fall on Adam, then He opened up his side, took out a rib, and closed his flesh up again. God formed Eve from the rib He had taken from Adam.)

3. What did Adam say when God brought Eve to him? ("This is now bone of my bones and flesh of my flesh. She shall be called Woman because she was taken out of man.")

4. What two "firsts" did God perform in Genesis 2:21-22? (He performed the first surgery and the first wedding ceremony.)

5. According to John 8:44, who is the father of lies? (Satan)

6. Of which tree in the garden of Eden were Adam and Eve not to eat? (The tree of the knowledge of good and evil.)

7. What are the three basic temptations Satan uses on all mankind? (1-Lust of the flesh, 2-Lust of the eye, 3- Pride of Life)

8. What does Ephesians 5:25 tell us that wives are to do? (Wives are to submit to their husbands.)

9. How does sin affect our relationship with God? (Sin separates us from God.)

10. Who does Adam try to blame for his sin? (He tries to blame Eve and even God for giving her to Adam.)

11. Who does Eve try to blame for her sin? (She tries to blame the serpent for deceiving her.)

12. Why is Genesis 3:15 a very important verse in the Bible? (It is the first prophecy of the coming Savior, Jesus Christ.)

13. What was Eve's punishment (or curse)? (She would have pain in childbirth, and her husband would rule over her.)

14. What does Eve's name mean? ("Mother of all living")

15. What was the name of Eve's first son? (Cain)

16. What was the name of Eve's second son? (Abel)

17. What happened to her second son? (He was killed by his older brother.)

18. What was the name of Eve's third son? (Seth)

19. What does his name mean? (Appointed)

20. Name some "firsts" that Eve experienced. (She was the first woman, first wife, first mother, first sinner. She was in the first wedding. She was first to experience the grief of losing a loved one. She witnessed the first sacrifice and heard the first hope of salvation from God. Other answers may also apply.)

* **"Finish the Family"** –1) Noah, Shem, Ham, <u>Japheth</u> 2) Eunice, <u>Lois</u>, Timothy 3) Jacob, Leah, Reuben, Simeon, Levi, Judah, <u>Issachar</u>, Zebulun, Dinah 4) <u>Zebedee</u>, James, John 5) Joseph, Asenath, <u>Manasseh</u>, Ephraim 6) Boaz, Ruth, <u>Obed</u> 7) Abraham, <u>Sarah</u>, Isaac 8) Joab, Abishai, <u>Asahel</u> 9) <u>Eliab</u>, Abinadab, Shimea, Nethanel, Raddai, Ozem, Zeruiah, David 10) Aaron, <u>Miriam</u>, Moses

  #1 is a father and sons, #2 is a mother, grandmother, and son/grandson, #3 is a husband, wife, and children, #4 is a father and his two sons, #5 is a husband, wife, and two sons, #6 is a husband, wife, and son, #7 is a husband, wife, and son, #8 is three brothers who were nephews of king David, #9 is seven brothers and one sister (king David's brothers and his sister, Zeruiah – #8 are her three sons), #10 is a brother, sister, and brother.

- Mystery Math –

1. On which day of creation was Eve created by God? **6**

2. How many children of Eve are named in Genesis 4? **3**

   Divide the answer to #1 by the answer to #2. **2**

3. How many are included in the Godhead referred to in Genesis 1? **3**

   Add the answer to #3 to the last answer to #2. **5**

4. How many people ate of the forbidden fruit? **2**

   Add the answer to #4 to the last answer to #3. **7**

5. On which day of creation would dinosaurs have been created? **6**

   Subtract the answer to #5 from the last answer to #4. **1**

   What is the final number? **1**
   God said that when a man and a woman were joined together in marriage, they would be __one__. (Genesis 2:24)

Lesson 2:

Review Questions:

1. What tribe of Israel were Amram and Jochebed from? (The tribe of Levi)

2. How many children did they have, and what were their names? (Three – Miriam, Aaron and Moses)

3. Why did the Pharaoh of Egypt make the Israelites slaves? (He was afraid of them because there were so many of them. He thought he could keep them under his control if he enslaved them.)

4. What terrible command did the Pharaoh issue in Exodus 1:22? (He commanded that all of the Hebrew baby boys be thrown into the river.)

5. What unusual thing did Jochebed do with her baby boy for the first three months after he was born? (She hid him.)

6. What materials did Jochebed use to fashion a little waterproof ark for her baby? (She wove bulrushes together and daubed the ark with pitch.)

7. After the baby was placed inside, where was the ark placed? (In the river near the water's edge.)

8. Who remained close by to watch over the baby and to see what would happen? (His sister, Miriam)

9. Why did the daughter of Pharaoh come down to the river? (She came to the river to bathe.)

10. When her maid brought her the ark and opened it, what did the baby do? (He cried.)

11. What was the reaction of the princess to this? (She felt compassion for the baby.)

12. What did Miriam boldly offer the princess? (She offered to go and find a Hebrew nurse for the child.)

13. Who was selected for this position? (Jochebed)

14. What does the name Moses mean? ("Drawn out")

15. Did Moses realize he was a Hebrew? (Yes)

- Word Scramble - 1) Levi, 2) Hebrews, 3) Jochebed, 4) Amram, 5) daughter, 6) Miriam, 7) bulrushes, 8) beautiful, 9) three, 10) faith

- What's Wrong with this Picture? -

Levi

A man from the tribe of Levi took as a wife a daughter of ~~Judah~~. They had a beautiful

three

little boy whom they hid from Pharaoh for ~~four~~ months. When his mother could no

bulrushes

longer hide him, she made a small ark of ~~pine needles~~ and daubed it with pitch. She river   sister

placed the baby in the basket and placed him in the ~~Red Sea~~. His ~~brother~~ stood nearby

to see what would happen. The daughter of Pharaoh came down to the water to wash ~~her~~

herself

~~clothes~~, and she saw the basket. One of her maids brought it to her, and when she

cried   sister   nurse

opened it, the baby ~~laughed~~. The baby's ~~brother~~ asked her if she would like a ~~doctor~~ for

Go

the child, and she said, "~~Yes~~." The baby's real mother was chosen to nurse him, then he

was brought to Pharaoh's daughter to become her son. She named him Moses which

the water

means he was taken out of ~~a basket~~.

Lesson 3:

Review Questions:

1. How many spies did Joshua send out to view the land? (Two)

2. On which side of the Jordan River were the Israelites encamped at this time? (The east side in Acacia Grove)

3. Who was informed that there were spies in the city staying at the house of Rahab? (The king of Jericho)

4. What did he do with this information? (He ordered Rahab to bring the spies out.)

5. Where did Rahab say the spies were? (She said they had already left the city.)

6. Where did Rahab hide the spies? (She hid them on her roof underneath some stalks of drying flax.)

7. How far did the men of Jericho go in trying to track down the spies? (They went all the way to the fords of the Jordan.)

8. How did Rahab describe the feelings of the people of Jericho and all of Canaan concerning the Israelites? (They were all terrified and had no courage.)

9. Rahab told the spies that she had heard what the God of Israel had done for His people. What three events did she mention? (The crossing of the Red Sea, the defeat of Sihon and the defeat of Og, kings of the Amorites)

10. What request did Rahab make of the spies? (She asked them to spare her life and the lives of her family when the Israelites conquered the city and land.)

11. Did the spies agree to her request? (Yes, but on the condition that they all keep silent about the spies and what they were doing.)

12. How did the spies leave Jericho without detection? (Rahab let them down the outside wall by a rope hanging from her window.)

13. How long did Rahab tell the spies to hide in the mountains? (Three days)

14. What two conditions did the spies give Rahab in order for them to keep their promise to her? (They told her to hang a scarlet cord in the window of her house and to bring all of her family that she wanted to be saved into her house.)

15. What condition would allow the spies to break this promise? (If any of her family members went outside the protection of her house, then the spies would not be responsible for any harm or death that might occur to that person. Also, if any of them did not keep silent about the spies and their mission, then the spies would no longer be bound to their promise.)

16. Did Rahab agree to everything the spies told her to do? (Yes)

© 2018, Pryor Convictions Media, Paul & Heather Pryor, St. Petersburg, FL

17. What did Rahab do as soon as the spies left her home? (She tied the scarlet cord in her window.)

18. Where did the spies go after leaving Rahab's house? (They went and hid in the mountains as she had instructed them.)

19. When they returned to the Israelite camp, whom did they report to? (Joshua)

20. Give a brief summary of their report. (They told Joshua that everyone in the country was terrified of them, and that the Lord was going to give them success in taking the land.)

21. When Joshua and the Israelites conquered the city of Jericho, were the promises by Rahab and the spies kept? (Yes)

22. What New Testament verse tells us that Rahab acted in faith? (Hebrews 11:31)

• Research – 1) Salmon, 2) Judah, 3) Boaz, 4) Ruth, 5) David

• Who Said It? - 1) Rahab, 2) Two spies, 3) Joshua, 4) Two spies, 5) Rahab, 6) King of Jericho, 7) Rahab, 8) Two spies, 9) Jericho citizens, 10) Rahab

• True or False? - 1) True, 2) True, 3) False, 4) True, 5) False, 6) False, 7) True, 8) False, 9) True, 10) True

Lesson 4:

Review Questions:

1. What number judge was Deborah out of the 15 judges of Israel? (She was the 4th judge.)

2. What are three things we know about Deborah? (1-She was married to a man named Lapidoth. 2-She was a prophetess. 3-She had a judgment seat where she sat under a palm tree between Ramah and Bethel.)

3. How long had King Jabin been oppressing Israel? (20 years)

4. What was the name of Jabin's general? (Sisera)

5. What was the name of Deborah's general? (Barak)

6. How many men of Israel were called to battle? (10,000)

7. What two tribes of Israel did these soldiers come from? (Naphtali and Zebulun)

8. How many chariots of iron did King Jabin have? (900)

9. Who was Heber the Kenite's wife? (Jael)

10. Which army was successful in the battle, the Israelites or the Canaanites, and why? (The Israelites were successful because the Lord was on their side and fought for them.)

11. Where did Sisera escape to? (He fled to the tent of Heber and Jael.)

12. What did Jael give him to drink? (Milk)

13. What did Sisera do next? (He laid down and slept.)

14. What happened to him at this time? (Jael crept up to him and drove a tent peg through his head, killing him.)

15. Who arrived at Heber's tent and found out what had happened? (Barak)

Research:
- The Song of Deborah – 1) The Lord, 2) The earth trembled, the clouds poured water, and the mountains gushed, 3) A mother in Israel, 4) Issachar and Reuben, 5) Dan and Asher, 6) Zebulun and Naphtali, 7) Jael, 8) Sisera's mother, 9) The sun in its full strength, 10) 40 years

- Crossword -

- Matching – 1) B, 2) H, 3) A, 4) J, 5) D, 6) C, 7) I, 8) E, 9) F, 10) G

Lesson 5:

Review Questions:

1. Which tribe of Israel did Elkanah belong to? (Ephraim)

2. What is polygamy? (Polygamy is having more than one wife.)

3. Who were Eli's two sons? (Hophni and Phinehas)

4. What was the Jewish center of worship which was located in Shiloh? (The tabernacle)

5. At the yearly sacrifice in Shiloh, what did Elkanah give to Hannah? (He gave her a double portion of food, more than he had given his other wife.)

6. Describe Peninnah's treatment of Hannah. (Peninnah tormented or provoked Hannah constantly because Hannah was childless. She is called Hannah's rival or adversary meaning she was Hannah's enemy.)

7. Why did Elkanah think Hannah should not be upset? (He thought she shouldn't be sad over what she did not have but should be happy about what she did have. She had a husband who loved her dearly, and he thought it should be enough for her.)

8. When Hannah was in anguish and "bitterness of soul", what did she do? (She prayed to God.)

9. What promise did Hannah make to the Lord? (She vowed that if God would bless her with a son, she would give the son back to God to be in His service all the days of his life.)

10. What was a Nazirite? (A Nazirite was someone who was set apart for service to God either for a certain period of their life or for their whole life. They had special rules to follow such as not allowing a razor to touch their head.)

11. What did Eli think of Hannah when she was at the door of the tabernacle, and why did he think this? (He thought she was drunk because he only saw her lips moving. He could not hear her praying as she was doing it silently.)

12. What did Eli tell Hannah after she explained to him about her prayer to God? (He told her to go in peace, that God had heard her prayer and would answer.)

13. How did Hannah leave Shiloh? (She left peacefully and was no longer sad.)

14. What scripture in the New Testament tells us not to be anxious and how to have peace in our hearts? (Philippians 4:6-7)

15. What does it mean in the Bible whenever it says the Lord remembers someone? (It means He is about to do something for them.)

16. What does Samuel's name mean? (It means "asked of the Lord.")

17. Why did Hannah not go to Shiloh after Samuel was born? (She was waiting until she had weaned the child before taking him to Shiloh to present him to the Lord.)

18. Did Elkanah agree or disagree with Hannah's vow? (Agree)

19. Could Elkanah have canceled Hannah's vow if he had wanted to? (Yes)

© 2018, Pryor Convictions Media, Paul & Heather Pryor, St. Petersburg, FL

20. In whose care did Hannah leave Samuel as he grew and served the Lord? (Eli's)

21. How often did Hannah see Samuel after leaving him in Shiloh? (She saw him once a year.)

22. What did she bring him at each visit? (A little robe to wear)

23. What blessing did Eli pray for Elkanah and Hannah each time they visited Shiloh? (He prayed that the Lord would bless them with more children to reward her for giving Samuel to the Lord's service.)

24. How many other children did the Lord bless Hannah with? (Five - Three sons and two daughters)

25. Write I Samuel 2:26. ("*And the child Samuel grew in stature, and in favor both with the Lord and men.*")

- Before or After? - 1) After, 2) After, 3) Before, 4) Before, 5) After, 6) Before, 7) Before, 8) After, 9) After, 10) Before

Lesson 6:

Review Questions:

1. What is wisdom? (Wisdom is the ability to make right decisions and use good judgment.)

2. Where was the queen of Sheba from? (We don't know for certain. Jesus called her "the queen of the South". Two likely locations are Ethiopia or Arabia.)

3. What gifts did the queen of Sheba bring for the king? (Spices, gold and precious stones)

4. How many of the queen of Sheba's questions was Solomon unable to answer? (None. He was able to answer all of them.)

5. After hearing the wisdom of Solomon, what did he show the queen of Sheba? (He showed her his house that he had built, the food which was served on his table, his servants, and his entryway to the temple from his house.)

6. What was the reaction of the queen of Sheba to all of this? (The Bible says, "There was no more spirit in her." She was completely overwhelmed by everything that she saw.)

7. How did Solomon show wisdom in the way he treated his servants? (He dressed them richly and fed them good food. Servants who are well cared-for are usually faithful and dedicated to their master, doing their work well.)

8. How did the queen of Sheba describe the servants of Solomon? (Happy and blessed)

9. The queen of Sheba acknowledged that the Lord made Solomon king and gave two reasons why. What were they? (1-That Solomon would do justice, and 2- That he would do righteousness.)

10. What gifts did the queen of Sheba give to king Solomon before she returned home? (120 talents of gold, precious stones and spices)

11. What three items did Solomon's navy bring from the land of Ophir? (Gold, precious stones and almug wood)

12. What did Solomon use almug wood for? (He used it to make steps for the temple and his own house, as well as harps and stringed instruments.)

13. What gifts did Solomon give the queen of Sheba before she returned home? (He gave her anything she asked for.)

14. What Old Testament verse and what New Testament verse tell us that God gives wisdom? (Proverbs 2:6, James 1:5)

15. Who wrote the book of Proverbs? (Solomon)

- Crossword Puzzle -

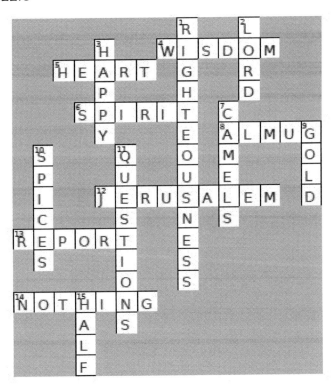

- Synonyms/Antonyms of Wisdom -

Synonyms	Antonyms
good judgment	ignorance
reason	stupidity
discernment	foolishness
prudence	nonsense
experience	inability
understanding	bad judgment

Lesson 7:

Review Questions:

1. What does "hospitality" mean? (Hospitality is to receive guests, visitors, or strangers to our home in a friendly and generous way.)

2. How is the Shunammite woman described? (A notable or great woman)

3. How did the Shunammite woman show hospitality to Elisha at first? (She would invite him to her home and fix a meal for him every time he came to town.)

4. How did she describe Elisha to her husband? (A holy man of God)

5. What four items did she include in the room for Elisha? (A bed, a table, a chair, and a lampstand)

6. What did Elisha first offer to do for her in order to show her thanks for her hospitality? (He offered to speak to the king on her behalf.)

7. Why did the Shunammite woman not accept Elisha's offer of him speaking to the king on her behalf? (She lived in peace among her neighbors and didn't need Elisha to speak to the king about anything.)

8. Who was Gehazi, and what did he suggest? (He was Elisha's servant who suggested that the Shunammite woman would like to have a child.)

9. What was the reaction of the Shunammite woman to the prophecy of Elisha? (She was shocked and didn't believe it.)

10. Did the prophecy of Elisha concerning the Shunammite woman come true? (Yes)

- Hosts and Hostesses – 1) Abraham, 2) Island Natives, 3) Zaccheus, 4) Pharaoh, 5) Rahab, 6) Lot, 7) Lydia, 8) Publius, 9) Martha, 10) Philippian Jailer

- Sequence – 1) **5**, 2) **1**, 3) **4**, 4) **8**, 5) **10**, 6) **2**, 7) **6**, 8) **9**, 9) **7**, 10) **3**

Lesson 8:

Review Questions:

1. Who was Athaliah's husband? (Jehoram)

2. Who were Athaliah's parents? (Ahab & Jezebel)

3. Who was Athaliah's son? (Ahaziah)

4. Which kingdom did her husband and son reign over? (The southern kingdom of Judah)

5. What kind of king was Ahaziah (good or evil), and who gave him advice on how to reign? (He was an evil king whose mother counseled him to do wickedly.)

6. How long did Ahaziah reign as king? (One year)

7. What was the first thing Athaliah did after her son had died? (She destroyed all the royal heirs to the throne.)

8. Who was Joash, and what did Jehoshabeath do to him? (Joash was one of the king's sons. Jehoshabeath hid him to protect him from Athaliah.)

9. Who was Jehoshabeath's father? (King Jehoram) Brother? (King Ahaziah) Husband? (Jehoiada the priest)

10. How long was Joash hidden, and where was he hidden? (He was hidden for six years in the temple.)

11. Who ruled over the nation of Judah during this time? (Athaliah)

12. Which king was Joash a direct descendant of? (David)

13. What had God promised this king over one hundred years earlier? (God had promised David that he would always have a descendant on the throne.)

14. Who did Jehoiada place around the king to guard him? (The Levites)

15. What did they have in their hands? (Weapons)

16. On what day of the week was Joash crowned king? (He was crowned on the Sabbath day which was Saturday.)

17. After the crown was placed on his head, what was given to Joash? (A copy of the law of Moses)

18. What did the people cry out when Joash was anointed king? ("Long live the king!")

19. What did Athaliah cry out when she discovered what was going on? ("Treason! Treason!")

20. What happened to Athaliah the day Joash was crowned king? (She was executed.)

21. What was the covenant the people made after Athaliah had died? (They agreed to follow the Lord faithfully.)

22. What false god did Athaliah worship? (Baal)

23. What did the people tear down in the city? (They tore down the temple of Baal.)

24. Who was executed there? (Mattan, a priest of Baal)

25. What was the reaction of the people to Joash taking his place on the throne and Athaliah's death? (They rejoiced.)

- Before or After? – 1) After, 2) After, 3) Before, 4) After, 5) Before, 6) Before, 7) After, 8) After, 9) Before, 10) Before

- Who Am I? - 1) Jehoshabeath, 2) Ahaziah, 3) Omri, 4) Athaliah, 5) Jehoiada, 6) Joash, 7) Jehoram, 8) Ahab, 9) David, 10) Mattan

Lesson 9:

Review Questions:

1. Whose mother taught him the importance of a virtuous wife? (King Lemuel)

2. What is a virtuous wife worth to her husband? (More than rubies)

3. What will a virtuous wife do for her husband all the days of his life? (Good)

4. In what way did the virtuous woman work with her hands? (Willingly)

5. What time did the virtuous woman get up each day? (While it was still night)

6. What did the virtuous woman buy with her profits, and what did she plant? (She bought a field and planted a vineyard.)

7. How did the virtuous woman treat the poor and needy? (With compassion)

8. What does the word *scarlet* refer to? (Double thickness of cloth)

9. What did the virtuous woman decorate her home with? (Tapestries)

10. What was her clothing made out of? (Fine linen and purple)

11. Where did her husband sit each day? (Among the elders of the land)

12. What did the virtuous woman sell? (Linen garments and sashes)

13. How did the virtuous woman view the future? (She rejoiced over it or laughed at it.)

14. What did she open her mouth with? (Wisdom)

15. How did she speak to others? (With kindness)

16. What did the virtuous woman never eat? (The bread of idleness)

17. What did the virtuous woman's children call her? (Blessed)

18. How did the virtuous woman's husband feel about her? (He praised her.)

19. What does Proverbs 31:30 say is vain or useless? (Beauty)

20. What kind of woman will be praised? (One who fears the Lord)

- True or False: 1) True, 2) False, 3) False, 4) True, 5) False, 6) True, 7) False, 8) True, 9) False, 10) False

- Complete the proverb: 1) f, 2) j, 3) h, 4) g, 5) i, 6) a, 7) d, 8) c, 9) e, 10) b

Lesson 10:

Review Questions:

1. Who was Lot related to, and how were they related? (Lot was the nephew of Abraham.)

2. How many children did Lot and his wife have? (Two daughters)

3. Once Lot and his family were outside the city of Sodom, what instructions did the angels give them? (Escape for their lives, and do not look back.)

4. Where did Lot and his family escape to? (The city of Zoar)

5. What happened to Sodom and Gomorrah once Lot and his family were safely away? (The Lord rained down fire and brimstone on the cities to destroy them.)

6. What did Lot's wife do, and what happened to her as a result? (She disobeyed the Lord's command by looking back at the city of Sodom. She was immediately turned into a pillar of salt.)

7. Who gave a warning in Luke 17:32 to, *"Remember Lot's wife."*? (Jesus)

8. What kind of man was Job spiritually? (He was blameless and upright. He followed the Lord and turned away from evil.)

9. How many children did Job have? (He had seven sons and three daughters.)

10. Describe Job's wealth. (He had 7,000 sheep, 3,000 camels, 500 yoke of oxen and 500 female donkeys plus a large number of servants.)

11. What reason does Satan give the Lord for Job being such a righteous man before God? (He says it is because God blesses Job so much.)

12. What does Satan think Job will do if the Lord were to take everything away from him? (He thinks Job will curse God to His face.)

13. What does the Lord give Satan permission to do in their first conversation? (He allows Satan to do what he likes to all of Job's possessions, but he is not allowed to harm Job physically.)

14. How many messengers brought bad news to Job? (Four)

15. What was the last bit of bad news that Job received? (He was told that all of his children were killed.)

16. How much of Job's possessions were lost? (All of the animals were lost and most of the servants.)

17. What outward signs of grief did Job display? (He tore his robe and shaved his head.)

18. How did Job react to the Lord after receiving all of this bad news? (He worshiped God and blessed the name of the Lord. He didn't curse God or blame Him for any of it.)

19. How did Satan attack Job the second time? (He struck him with painful boils all over his body.)

20. What did Job do after this happened? (He sat in a pile of ashes and scraped himself with a potsherd.)

21. What did Job's wife want him to do? (She wanted him to curse God and die.)

22. How did Job answer her? (He told her she was talking foolishly.)

23. Who was Maacah's husband? (Rehoboam) Son? (Abijam) Grandfather? (Absalom)

24. What kind of king was Maacah's grandson, Asa? (He was a good king who followed the Lord.)

25. What position did Maacah hold in Asa's royal court? (She was the queen mother.)

26. What did Asa do to her? (He removed her from her position as queen mother.)

27. Why did Asa do this? (He did this because she had made an image of an idol. She was disobedient to the Lord.)

- Who Am I? - 1) Absalom, 2) Lot's wife, 3) Abraham, 4) Job's wife, 5) Maacah, 6) Asa, 7) angel, 8) Lot, 9) The Lord, 10) King David

Lesson 11:

Review Questions:

1. How did the Syro-Phoenician woman refer to Jesus? (She called him "Lord, Son of David".)

2. What was wrong with this woman's daughter? (Her daughter was demon-possessed.)

3. What was Jesus' first response to her? (He didn't answer her at all. He ignored her.)

4. What did the disciples ask Jesus to do and why? (They asked him to send the woman away because she kept crying out after them.)

5. To whom did Jesus say he was sent? (He said he was sent to the house of Israel.)

6. This woman was not a Jew. What group would she be in as a non-Jew? (Gentile)

7. What does persistence mean? (It means never giving up.)

8. After being told that he was only sent to the Jews, what did the woman do next? (She worshiped Jesus.)

9. After pleading for his help again, how did Jesus answer her? (He said it wasn't good to take the children's bread and throw it to the little dogs.)

10. Did the woman take his answer as an insult? (No)

11. What does humility mean? (Humility is to think of others above yourself.)

12. The woman admitted that what Jesus said was true, but what did she still ask for? (Crumbs)

13. What did Jesus praise her for? (Her great faith)

14. Jesus gave her the desire of her heart. What was it? (He healed her demon-possessed daughter.)

15. When did he do this? (At that very hour)

- Finish the Verse -
1. "Then she came and worshiped Him, saying, '<u>Lord, help Me!</u>'" (Matthew 15:25)

2. "And behold, a woman of Canaan, came from that region and cried out to Him, saying, 'Have mercy on me, O Lord, Son of David! My <u>daughter is severely demon-possessed</u>.'" (Matthew 15:22)

3. "Jesus answered and said to her, 'O woman, <u>great is your faith! Let it be to you as you desire.'</u> And her daughter was healed from that very hour." (Matthew 15:28)

4. "And His disciples came and urged Him, saying, '<u>Send her away, for she cries out after us.</u>'" (Matthew 15:23)

5. "And she said, 'True, Lord, yet even the little dogs <u>eat the crumbs which fall from their masters' table.</u>'" (Matthew 15:27)

- Sequence – 1) **8**, 2) **3**, 3) **10**, 4) **1**, 5) **5**, 6) **2**, 7) **6**, 8) **4**, 9) **7**, 10) **9**

Lesson 12:

Review Questions:

1. What did Ananias and Sapphira sell? (A piece of land)

2. What did they decide to do with the money from the sale? (They were going to give it to the church, but they decided to keep back part of it for themselves.)

3. What sin did Peter accuse Ananias of? (Lying)

4. Was it wrong of Ananias and Sapphira to keep back part of the money from their sale? (No)

5. Who did Peter say had put this sin into the heart of Ananias? (Satan)

6. Who does John 8:44 refer to as "*the father of lies*"? (Satan)

7. What happened to Ananias as a result of his sin? (He fell down dead instantly.)

8. Did Sapphira know what had happened to her husband? (No)

9. How long was it from the time Ananias went to Peter and the time Sapphira went to him? (3 hours)

10. Did Sapphira have a chance to do what was right? (Yes)

11. What choice did she make, and what was the result? (She chose to lie as her husband did, and as a result, she fell down dead at the feet of Peter.)

12. Where was Sapphira buried? (Next to her husband)

13. What was the name of Priscilla's husband? (Aquila)

14. What trade did she and her husband work at? (They were tent-makers.)

15. Which apostle came to work and live with them for awhile? (Paul)

16. Who did Priscilla and her husband teach privately? (Apollos)

17. How did Paul describe Priscilla and her husband in Romans 16? (He called them "fellow workers in Christ Jesus".)

18. In what way had Priscilla and her husband helped Paul? (Paul said they had risked their necks for his life.)

19. What group met in the home of Priscilla and her husband? (A church)

20. Priscilla shows us an example of an excellent wife. How does Proverbs 12:4 describe a wife such as that? (She is the crown of her husband.)

- The Church - How many churches did Jesus say he would build? (Matthew 16:18) **One** *"My church"*, not churches; On what day was the first sermon preached and people were saved? (Acts 2:1, 40-41) **On the Day of Pentecost after the ascension of Christ** How were the people saved? (Acts 2:38; 41) **Through baptism for the remission of sins** Who adds people to the Lord's church? (Acts 2:47) **The Lord adds to the church those who are being saved.** Jesus said in John 4:24 that people needed to worship God in *"spirit and in truth"*. What acts of worship do we find in the New Testament that were practiced by the Lord's church? 1. **singing** (Eph. 5:19; Col. 3:16) There is no record anywhere in the New Testament of an instrument being used in the worship of the church. 2. **praying** (I Tim. 2:1-8) 3. **giving** (I Cor. 16:1-2; II Cor. 9:7) 4. **preaching the Word of God** (II Tim. 4:2; Acts 20:7) 5. **the Lord's Supper** (Acts 20:7; I Cor. 11:23-29)

- "Husbands and Wives" Matching - 1) e, 2) g, 3)h, 4) i, 5) a, 6) b, 7) j, 8) c, 9) f, 10) d

- What Happened Next? - 1) And breathed her last 2) They took him aside and explained to him the way of God more accurately. 3) But also all the churches of the Gentiles 4) And he kept back part of the proceeds, his wife also being aware of it, and brought a certain part and laid it at the apostles' feet. 5) And carrying her out, buried her by her husband 6) And upon all who heard these things 7) Fell down and breathed his last 8) He stayed with them and worked. 9) Though he knew only of the baptism of John 10) And the young men arose and wrapped him up, carried him out, and buried him.

Lesson 13:

Review Questions:

1. What city did Tabitha live in? (Joppa)

2. What was Tabitha's other name? (Dorcas)

3. What does the name "Tabitha" mean? (Gazelle)

4. What kind of woman was she? (A woman who was full of good works and charitable deeds.)

5. What happened to Tabitha? (She became sick and died.)

6. Where was her body laid? (In an upper room)

7. Who sent for Peter? (Some of the disciples)

8. Were they content to let Peter come whenever he was available? (No, they wanted him to come immediately.)

9. Who was in Tabitha's house weeping when Peter arrived? (Widows)

10. What had Tabitha made for them? (Clothing – tunics and garments)

11. After Peter knelt by Tabitha's bed and prayed, what did he say to her? ("Tabitha, arise.")

12. Who did Peter show Tabitha to after raising her from the dead? (The saints – fellow Christians)

13. What was the result of that miracle on the people in Joppa? (Many people believed on the Lord.)

14. Do we have any record of Tabitha's words? (No)

15. What does this woman of the Bible teach us? (Loving service)

- Word Scramble – 1) tunics, 2) disciple, 3) widows, 4) weeping, 5) Tabitha, 6) Joppa, 7) saints, 8) Lydda, 9) Peter, 10) prayed

- What's Missing? - 1) prayed, 2) Lydda, Joppa, Peter, 3) widows, weeping, 4) disciple, Tabitha, Dorcas, 5) saints, alive, 6) hand, lifted, 7) washed, upper, 8) woman, good, charitable, 9) sick, died, 10) believed, Lord

Appendix A - Maps

Map 1 - NE Egypt, Palestine & Mesopotamia

Map 2 - Egypt & Sinai Peninsula

Map 3 - Sinai Peninsula & Canaan

Map 4 - Israel

Map 5 - Israel & Syria

Map 6 - New Testament World

*Each map may be photocopied for personal home use as much as needed.

Map 1 – NE Egypt, Palestine & Mesopotamia

Map 2 – Egypt & Sinai Peninsula

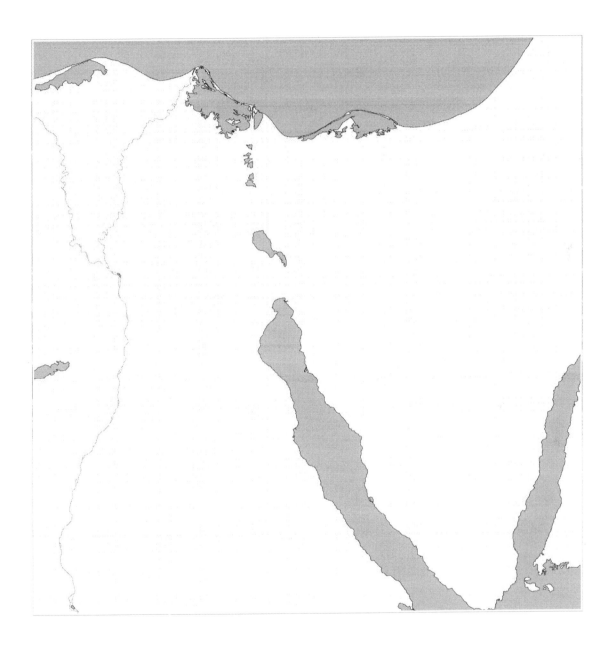

Map 3 - Sinai Peninsula & Canaan

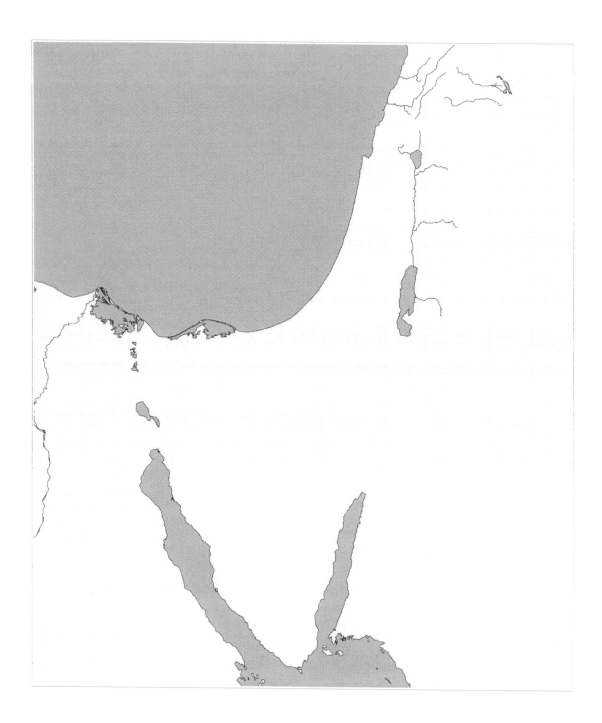

Map 4 - Israel

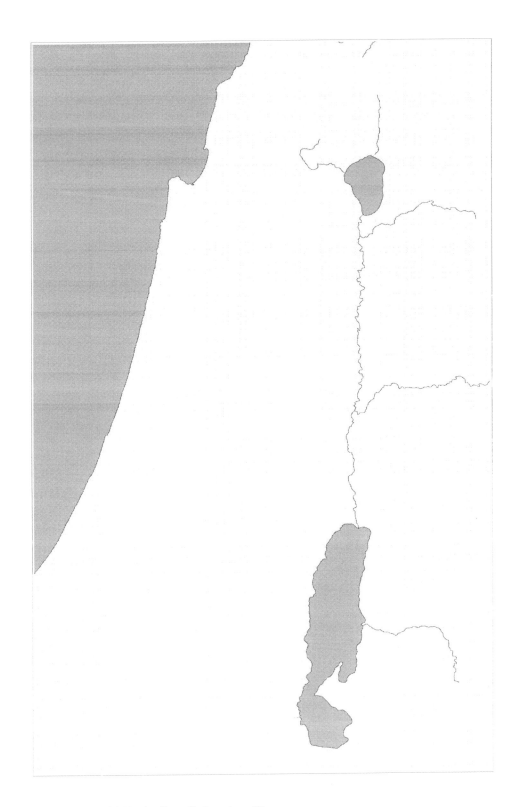

Map 5 – Israel & Syria

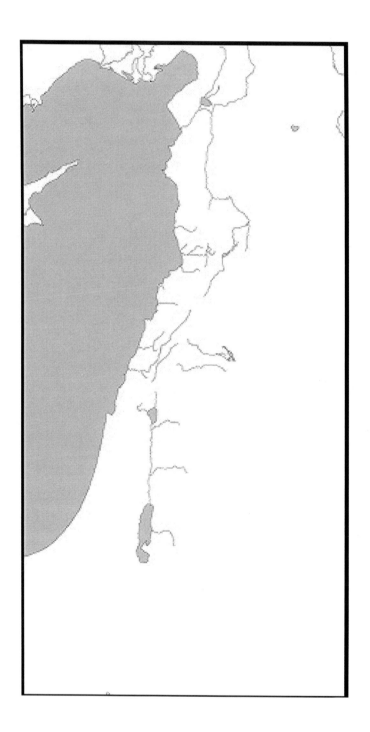

Map 6 – New Testament World

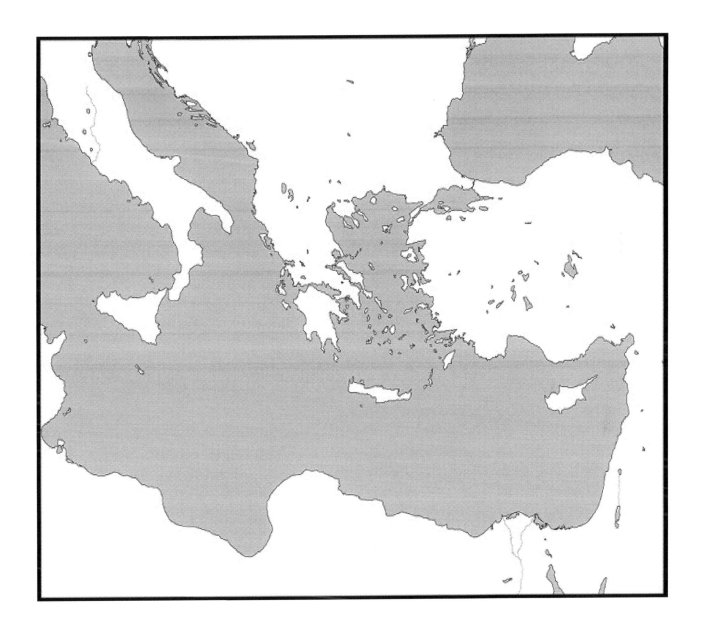

Appendix B – Templates

Lesson 1 – "Finish the Family" Template

Lesson 1 – Fill-in-the-blank names for "Finish the Family" Puzzle

Lesson 1 – Leaf Templates

Lesson 5 – Coat Template

Lesson 8 – Tea Label Templates

Lesson 12 – Priscilla/Sapphira Paper Doll Template

Lesson 13 – Heart Templates

*Each template may be photocopied for home use as much as needed.

Lesson 1 – "Finish the Family" Puzzle Template

1. Noah, Shem, Ham, _____

2. Eunice, _____, Timothy

3. Jacob, Leah, Reuben, Simeon, Levi, Judah, _____,
   Zebulun, Dinah

4. _____, James, John

5. Joseph, Asenath, _____, Ephraim

6. Boaz, Ruth, _____

7. Abraham, _____, Isaac

8. Joab, Abishai, _____

9. _____, Abinadab, Shimea, Nethanel, Raddai, Ozem,
   Zeruiah, David

10. Aaron, _____, Moses

Lesson 1 – Fill-in-the-blank names for "Finish the Family" Puzzle

Obed	Eliab
Manasseh	Miriam
Sarah	Japheth
Issachar	Lois
Asahel	Zebedee

Lesson 1 - Leaf Templates

Lesson 5 – Coat Template

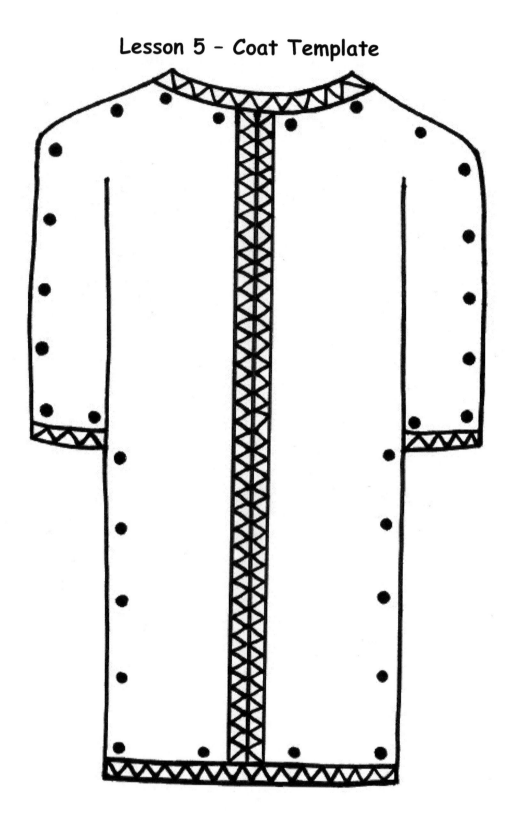

Lesson 8 – Tea Label Templates

Friendship

Tea Mix

To make tea: Place 4 1/2 tsp. of mix into tea cup. Pour boiling water over mix and stir well.

Chai Tea
Mix

To make tea: Place 2 heaping tsp. of mix into tea cup. Pour boiling water over mix and stir well.

Lesson 12 - Priscilla/Sapphira Paper Doll Template

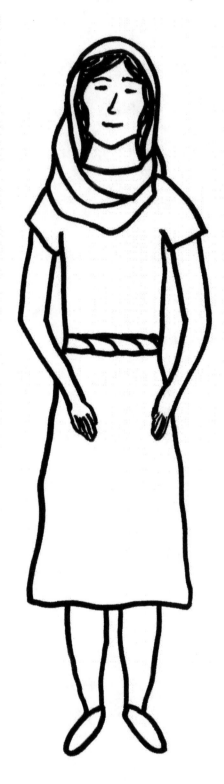

Lesson 13 - Heart Templates

Made in the USA
Middletown, DE
27 September 2023

39391405R00097